Checklist *for* My Family

A Guide to My History, Financial Plans, and Final Wishes

Sally Balch Hurme

Cover design by Jill Tedhams/ABA Publishing

21 20 19   13 12 11

Library of Congress Cataloging-in-Publication Data

Hurme, Sally Balch, author.
  ABA/AARP checklist for my family : a guide to my history, financial plans, and final wishes / by Sally Balch Hurme.
      pages cm
  Includes bibliographical references and index.
  ISBN 978-1-62722-982-1 (softcover : alk. paper) -- ISBN 978-1-62722-983-8 (e-book) 1. Estate planning--United States--Popular works. 2. Older persons--United States--Handbooks, manuals, etc.   I. American Bar Association. Senior Lawyers Division, sponsoring body. II. American Association of Retired Persons, sponsoring body. III. Title. IV. Title: Checklist for my family.
  KF750.Z9H87 2015
  332.024'0160973--dc23   2015002607

Discounts are available for books ordered in bulk. Special consideration is given to state bars, CLE programs, and other bar-related organizations. Inquire at Book Publishing, ABA Publishing, American Bar Association, 321 North Clark Street, Chicago, Illinois 60654.

AARP publishes a variety of books in print and electronic formats. Visit AARP.org/Bookstore.

www.ShopABA.org

TABLE OF CONTENTS

ABOUT THE AUTHOR

Sally Balch Hurme, J.D.

Sally Balch Hurme, J.D., is Project Advisor with the AARP Education & Outreach team. In her twenty-three years at AARP, she has advocated on a wide range of issues including consumer fraud, financial exploitation, elder abuse, surrogate decision making, advance care planning, predatory mortgage lending, health care fraud, and financial security. She is well recognized as an elder law advocate and is quoted frequently in national media including the *Wall Street Journal*, the *New York Times*, *USA Today*, CNN.com, *Money*, *Kiplinger's Retirement Report*, NPR, Sirius/XM Radio, and *AARP The Magazine*.

Although she has written more than twenty law review articles on elder law topics, she has focused her professional career on explaining the law so everyone can understand it. She has lectured on elder abuse and surrogate decision making in Japan, Australia, the Netherlands, Germany, Spain, Italy, Czech Republic, Great Britain, and Moldova. In 2010, she delivered an Honor Lecture at the World Congress on Adult Guardianship in Yokohama, Japan. She is also in demand as a speaker, having given over 100 presentations on elder law topics in at least 40 states.

For the past two decades her volunteer commitment has focused on the rights of adults with diminished capacity and the reform of guardianship policy and procedures. She has served multiple terms on the boards of the National Guardianship Association and the Center for Guardianship Certification, where she has been instrumental in developing standards for guardians and criteria to improve professional competency. Hurme is a past chair of the National Guardianship Network, a collaboration of eleven national organizations working to improve guardianship. She was an adviser to the Uniform Law Commission in the drafting of the Uniform Adult Guardianship and Protective Proceedings Jurisdiction Act, which has been quickly adopted in 39 states, the District of Columbia, and Puerto Rico. She was a member of U.S. State Department delegation to the Hague Conference on Private International Law that drafted the International Convention on the Protection of Incapacitated Adults. In 2008, she was honored by the National College of Probate Judges with the William Treat Award for excellence in probate law.

Hurme started her legal career as a partner in a private law firm, gained valuable experience serving older clients as a legal services attorney, and served as a magistrate in Alexandria, Virginia. She spent three years as an attorney adviser with the U.S. Department of Justice Office of Intelligence Policy and Review. She then returned to elder law advocacy as an assistant staff attorney with the American Bar Association Commission on Law and Aging before moving to AARP. Hurme taught elder law as an adjunct professor at the George Washington University Law School for eight years, honing her ability to explain the law. She is a long-term member of the National Academy of Elder Law Attorneys and the Virginia and District of Columbia bars. Hurme served as a member of the Discipline and Ethics Commission of the Certified Financial Planners Board of Standards. She is vice-chair of the Board of Governors of the Stuart Hall School in Staunton, Virgina.

She received her B.A. from Newcomb College of Tulane University, New Orleans, Louisiana, and received her J.D. *cum laude* from the Washington College of Law, American University, Washington, D.C. She lives in Alexandria, VA, but enjoys getaway time at her farms near Shepherdstown, West Virginia, and Bridgewater, Virginia.

INTRODUCTION
A FAMILY GIFT

For years, I put off getting organized: Typing up that list of passwords. Labeling those photos sitting in boxes on my bedroom floor. Updating my will.

It wasn't just that the chaos made me crazy. It was my concern that, should something happen to me, I was leaving my family in the dark.

If you're reading this book, there's a good chance that you, too, are ready to get your life in order and make sure your family knows your plans and wishes. That's where I step in: to make it easier and to nudge you each step of the way.

In the following pages, I guide you through the process of gathering in one place your finances, legal documents, online accounts, wishes about medical care, and more. Plus I tell you what you need, what's missing, and where to get it. While giving you peace of mind, this book is also a gift to your loved ones, sparing them stressful decisions and needless frustrations when you're ill or upon your death.

The chapters are arranged for you to set out your history, assets and liabilities, legal documents, and medical and final wishes.

In Chapter 1, you can provide your personal history, and in Chapter 2, you can outline your family history, sharing your memories and knowledge of those who came before you. Perhaps even more important to you and to your family than your passwords and bank statements is the cherished legacy you can provide by passing on your unique knowledge of your family history; your recollections about your own life, interests, and accomplishments; and other special remembrances.

In Chapters 3 through 8, you can detail your assets and liabilities to ease the process of handling your estate and make your family members aware of all the resources they may be entitled to. In Chapter 4, your family survivors will find checklists to help them apply for any benefits they are eligible to receive.

In Chapter 9, you can review the legal documents needed and note where they are located. This way, when the time comes, your loved ones will be able to locate the documents so important to you and to them.

In Chapter 10, you can set out what you would like your family to do when you are ill or upon your death. Many people live together for fifty years without discussing their wishes regarding life support, organ donations, funeral or memorial services, and burial or cremation. Without meaning to do so, they leave many distressing decisions for their loved ones. You can make it so much easier on your family during any illness and at your death by simply deciding on and putting in writing what you want and expect.

This book should bring both you and your family members comfort and peace of mind. They won't have to be scrambling to find documents or guessing what you might have wanted them to do. Filling out these checklists will make everyone's life so much easier.

How to use this book

Each chapter starts with a to-do checklist you can use as you collect the information you want to gather. For each item on the checklist, you will find basic information about it as well as tips on how to locate and organize it. After the explanations, you'll find action checklists where you provide your loved ones with a detailed record of your personal history, family history, financial assets, medical and final wishes, and other notes.

You probably can't complete this guide in one or two sittings. Some information will take extra thought or research. But don't look upon it as a task. If you approach it in manageable sections and view it as a fascinating family project, you will find great satisfaction in tracking down bits and pieces of your family history, locating the missing birth certificates, and gradually putting your affairs in order.

You will probably want to start by looking through the list of My To-Do Checklists starting on page xv to get an overview of the many topics covered by this book. Go through a first run to check off the items that don't apply to your circumstances. You may find that you'll want to start with just one section or checklist that is the easiest for you to accomplish.

Check off each item on the lists as you complete that step. Even though you might not have all the answers at first, take the time to find them. You will see tips on how to gather some of the information and places to record your information. You know the sources; your family may not.

You should also prioritize: What should be completed sooner rather than later? Your priority list is unique to you, but you may want to put at the top of your list having medical advance directives, recording your personal medication record, filling in your personal history, talking with your lawyer about your estate plans, indicating where your important papers are located, and making decisions about your funeral.

You are never too young or too old to make plans and arrangements so you can stay in control of your affairs. Accidents, strokes, heart attacks, and dementia can happen at any age, without warning. By starting now to plan ahead for possible incapacity and inevitable death, you are taking the positive steps to getting your life in order, reaching peace of mind, and ensuring your wishes are known.

Feel free to modify the checklists according to your needs. For example, if you are unmarried but have someone significant in your life that you would like to include, just cross through spouse and replace it with the term you prefer to describe your relationship, such as *special friend* or *lifetime partner*.

A few tips:

Fill in the paper checklists with a pencil or erasable pen. This book is for you to write in. If your decisions or assets change as time goes by, it will be easy to update what you have previously written.

Print legibly. After all, if you take the time to create this record, you want your family to be able to read it.

Keep the forms up-to-date. As changes occur, revise the forms. Update and review them at least once every year. Set aside some time at the beginning of each year to update the forms and add new information. Just after you have pulled together files and papers to prepare your taxes is a good time to review and update these forms.

Use the downloadable forms. The checklists in this book can be downloaded from the ABA website at (ambar.org/AARPforms). This makes it very easy for you to fill out the checklists and to make changes so they are up to date. Note in this book the file or folder name so your family can easily find it on your computer. As you complete a chapter, you may want to print out a copy and place the pages in a three-ring binder. You may also want to add plastic pages to slip in clippings or documents you come across. You'll want to keep a hard copy (and a backup file) of these documents in your filing system. Be sure to note where you have those copies stored so they will be readily available.

Discuss this book with your family members. They must be aware that you have taken the time to gather the valuable information in this book, know where your checklists are located, and be informed about your wishes. Be sure to tell them that you are working on gathering this information. Whether you are recording it in the book, storing it electronically, or printing out pages for a binder, your family needs to know how to locate this treasure trove of information.

A word of caution. You are assembling a great deal of very personal information that, in the wrong hands, could be used to your disadvantage. Unfortunately, there are unscrupulous people who do not have your best interests in mind. They may even be people you think you should be able to trust. While they may not admit it, some relatives may be more concerned about their own interests than yours. In some families, it is difficult to impossible to reach a consensus or agreement on just about anything. Be cautious about whom you share the information with. The nosy neighbor, the distant relative, or the casual friend may not be able to keep confidential this very private information.

A word of encouragement. These records can be of significant interest and value to you during your lifetime and can provide a sense of personal freedom. The greatest satisfaction will be in knowing that if anything happens to you, you will be providing an invaluable resource for your family with your notes, your wishes, and the information in this book.

CHECKLISTS

My To-Do Checklists

Personal History

- ✔ Get copies of birth certificate
- ✔ Get copies of marriage license
- ✔ Get copies of adoption papers
- ✔ Get copies of citizenship/naturalization documents
- ✔ Get copies of divorce decree
- ✔ Complete Personal Medication Record
- ✔ Organize tax files by year
- ✔ List all employers
- ✔ Keep original documents that are valuable or irreplaceable in a safe deposit box

Family History

- ✔ Take advantage of family gatherings or reunions to get help compiling family history information
- ✔ Complete the Family Medical History Checklist

Insurance

- ✔ Review the terms of all insurance policies
- ✔ Locate all insurance policies
- ✔ Update the beneficiaries you have listed on your policies
- ✔ Annually review your health, disability, Medicare, and long-term care insurance options
- ✔ Keep vehicle insurance current
- ✔ Review homeowners and renters insurance coverage

Retirement and Veterans Benefits

✔ Assess Social Security benefits for you and your survivors

✔ Check out benefits for veterans and their survivors

✔ Record any workers' compensation benefits

✔ Identify all available pension benefits

✔ Identify your retirement plans

✔ Verify and update the beneficiary designation on pension and retirement plans

Banking and Saving

✔ Review how bank accounts are titled

✔ List all banks where you do business

✔ List any credit unions where you do business

✔ Assemble account numbers and—with caution—your access PINs, ATM passwords, online banking usernames and passwords

✔ Keep a record of all savings bonds

✔ Make sure that your accounts are FDIC insured

✔ Keep original documents that are valuable or irreplaceable in a safe deposit box

✔ Be sure that someone knows where safe deposit boxes and keys are located

Investments

✔ Periodically check to make sure your investments match your investment objectives and are diversified

✔ Check on the background of any financial professional

✔ Organize statements you receive from your brokerage firm or investment adviser

Real Estate

✔ Assemble copies of the deeds to all real estate

✔ Review how your property is titled

✔ Discuss your real estate ownership and taxes with a tax adviser or estate planner

✔ Determine if your property qualifies for tax relief

✔ Consolidate all investment and commercial property records

✔ Obtain a copy of your Master Deed and condominium association documents

✔ Obtain a copy of your timeshare contract

Other Assets and Debts

✔ Assemble receipts or appraisals for higher-valued possessions

✔ Photograph or videotape special possessions

✔ Write down stories about how you acquired special possessions

✔ Label the photographs

✔ Inventory your digital assets

✔ Put the terms of any personal loans in writing

✔ List contact information for credit cards

✔ Note if you have a reverse mortgage

Wills, Trusts, and Powers of Attorney

✔ Consult with an estate planning expert

✔ Consult with a tax adviser

✔ Document any major financial gifts

✔ Identify a source of funding for costs to close the estate

✔ Prepare or review your will

✔ Prepare any necessary codicils to your will

✔ Consider if a living trust should be part of your estate plan

✔ Select an agent to manage your financial affairs

✔ Prepare a letter of instruction

✔ Discuss your plan with those who need to know

Medical and Final Wishes

✔ Select the person you want to be your health care agent

✔ Consider preparing an ethical will

✔ Prepare an organ donor card

✔ Plan the disposition of your body

✔ Plan your funeral

✔ Consider options for paying for your funeral

✔ Plan your final resting place

✔ Know your veterans burial benefits

My Action Checklists

I have completed the following forms for my family:

Personal History

- ☐ Personal History
- ☐ Awards
- ☐ Biography
- ☐ Contacts
- ☐ Education
- ☐ Employment
- ☐ Memberships
- ☐ Personal Medication Record
- ☐ Pets
- ☐ Religion, Politics, and Hobbies
- ☐ Residences
- ☐ Where to Find It

Family History

- ☐ Children
- ☐ Parents
- ☐ Brothers and Sisters
- ☐ Grandparents
- ☐ Aunts, Uncles, and Cousins
- ☐ Stepparents
- ☐ Stepbrothers and Stepsisters
- ☐ Stepgrandparents
- ☐ Family Medical History

Insurance

- ☐ Annuity
- ☐ Health Insurance: Disability, Medicare, Long-Term Care
- ☐ Homeowners and Renters Insurance
- ☐ Life Insurance
- ☐ Umbrella Insurance Policy
- ☐ Vehicle Insurance

Retirement and Veterans Benefits

- ☐ Pensions
- ☐ Retirement Plans
- ☐ Social Security Benefits
- ☐ Veterans Benefits
- ☐ Workers' Compensation

Banking and Savings

- ☐ Certificates of Deposit
- ☐ Checking Accounts
- ☐ Credit Unions
- ☐ Safe Deposit Boxes
- ☐ Savings Accounts
- ☐ Savings Bonds

Investments

- ☐ Bonds
- ☐ College Savings Plan (529 Plans)
- ☐ Money Market Funds
- ☐ Municipal Bonds
- ☐ Mutual Funds
- ☐ Stocks
- ☐ Treasury Bills and Bonds

Real Estate

- ☐ Business
- ☐ Condominium
- ☐ Farm Land
- ☐ Investment
- ☐ Primary Residence
- ☐ Rental Residence
- ☐ Secondary Residence
- ☐ Timeshare
- ☐ Trust

Other Assets and Debts

- ☐ Business Interests
- ☐ Collectibles
- ☐ Copyrights, Patents, and Royalties
- ☐ Credit/Debit Cards
- ☐ Digital Assets
- ☐ Lawsuits and Judgments
- ☐ Outstanding Loans
- ☐ Personal Debt
- ☐ Personal Property
- ☐ Reverse Mortgage
- ☐ Rewards Programs
- ☐ Storage Units
- ☐ Vehicles

Wills, Trusts, and Powers of Attorney

- ☐ Codicils
- ☐ Durable Power of Attorney
- ☐ Gifts
- ☐ Letter of Instruction
- ☐ Living Trust
- ☐ Will

Medical and Final Wishes

- ☐ Burial
- ☐ Celebration of Life
- ☐ Charities
- ☐ Cremation
- ☐ Donation of Organs and Tissues
- ☐ Entombment
- ☐ Ethical Will/Legacy Documents
- ☐ Final Wishes
- ☐ Funeral
- ☐ Health Care Directives
- ☐ Items to Destroy
- ☐ Letters to Friends and Relatives
- ☐ Memorial Service
- ☐ Obituary
- ☐ People to Contact
- ☐ Pet Care
- ☐ Veterans Burial Benefits
- ☐ Whole Body Donation

PDF versions of these checklists can be found at ambar.org/AARPforms.

CHAPTER 1
PERSONAL HISTORY

*We can only be said to be alive
in those moments when our hearts
are conscious of our treasures.*

—Thornton Wilder

No one knows your personal history as well as you do. Chances are good that your children, family, and significant others may not know as much about you as you might think.

Even if some of your immediate family does know all about your personal history, you'll find many benefits to taking the time to record the details. You can make sure that the information passed on to later generations is accurate. And you may also enjoy tracking down bits of information and remembering key events in your life:

- Where you were born
- Where you went to school
- Where you have lived
- The different types of work experiences you have had
- The hobbies and activities you have enjoyed through the years

Haven't you asked yourself many of these questions in regard to your parents or grandparents? Most of us become more interested in family history as we grow older, but unless someone records that history for us, it will be lost. *You* are the one who can do this best for your family.

My To-Do Checklist

Done   Need to Do

Done	Need to Do	
☐	☐	Get copies of birth certificate
☐	☐	Get copies of marriage license
☐	☐	Get copies of adoption papers
☐	☐	Get copies of citizenship/naturalization documents
☐	☐	Get copies of divorce decree
☐	☐	Complete Personal Medication Record
☐	☐	Organize tax files by year
☐	☐	List all employers
☐	☐	Keep original documents that are valuable or irreplaceable in a safe deposit box
☐	☐	Complete the checklists for Chapter 1

The checklists in Chapter 1 seek detailed information about you—your educational background, where you have lived and worked, organizations you have belonged to, awards you have received. You also have space to record information about your pets, religious or political activities, and hobbies. You will find useful tips for tracking down any missing documentation.

Use the Contacts Checklist to record in one convenient place the contact information for all the people you rely on and with whom your family may need to get in touch. You should have fun filling out the Records Checklist pages. Where *have* you put the keys to your safe deposit box and what's the combination for the lock on your extra storage shed? Let someone know where you are keeping important papers. You never know when your family will need to find a copy of your contract for your security system or your home-owner's insurance policy. In other chapters you can record more information about these various documents.

Don't overlook the Personal Medication Record. You should carry a copy of this page with you in your wallet in case of emergency. Having all your medications and allergies on one form will come in handy when you go to your doctors, too.

Finally, you will find a page entitled "Other." This is for you to fill in with personal notes about yourself—your interests, accomplishments, thoughts, or desires. Add anything you consider to be of interest to your family. Don't be modest! If you did something in your lifetime for which you are proud, tell them about it. They will be proud, too. If something very humorous happened to you, they will enjoy it. Remember how you were fascinated with the interesting stories told to you by your mother, father, and grandparents? Your family members are just as interested in your remembrances.

At the time of your death, some of this information you record in these checklists can be used in the preparation of a death certificate, newspaper obituary, estate and income tax returns, and many other documents, as well as applying for survivors' benefits.

✔ **Get copies of birth certificate**

✔ **Get copies of marriage license**

✔ **Get copies of adoption papers**

Your family will need these documents to settle your estate and apply for various benefits. You need to record where you have stored your certificates or start the process now to obtain copies. While you are tracking down your own certificates, you may also want to obtain copies of certificates for your family members, so they'll be on hand whenever needed.

Where can you find them? The vast majority of births, deaths, and marriages are reported to the proper local authorities to maintain a lasting record. However, for a number of reasons, you or your heirs may have difficulty or encounter delay obtaining these records if you have not put them where they can readily find them. For example, in the not-too-distant past, many births occurred in private homes and went unrecorded. Occasionally, fire destroys courthouses or other record depositories. Records may be incorrect because of misspelling, changes in spelling, illegible handwriting, misunderstanding of names, and other errors.

You should obtain copies of any adoption papers, too. In some instances, it may be rather complicated to get information about some adoptions, depending on the circumstances.

Obtain and keep in a safe deposit box two *certified* copies each of birth and marriage certificates for you, your spouse, and your children. To be a "certified copy," it must have a statement by an official that it is a true copy of an original.

Each state has its own method of maintaining these records. Birth and marriage certificates can usually be obtained from the county clerk, registrar, or recorder of the county in which the birth or marriage took place.

Many states have a central clearing house generally called the Department of Vital Statistics. The Centers for Disease Control and Prevention has a useful website with information on how and where to write or call to obtain these records in each state at www.cdc.gov /nchs/w2w.htm.

Fees generally range from $2 to $20 for each certificate. Additional copies may be available at reduced rates. Once you know the cost, to speed up the process you can enclose the necessary payment when you write for the copies you need.

Many states will not issue copies of birth or marriage certificates unless the requestor is closely related to the person named in the certificate. Therefore, it is important to identify yourself as spouse, parent, or child when requesting records for someone else in your family.

✔ Get copies of citizenship/naturalization documents

If you have lost or can't find your citizenship/naturalization documents, you can request replacement copies from the U.S. Citizenship and Immigration Services. You'll need form N-565. Download a copy of the form at www.uscis.gov/n-565.

✔ Get copies of divorce decree

Your family will also need certified copies of judgments of divorce or annulment to apply for Social Security death or survivor benefits, veterans benefits, and private pension plans. You obtain them from the clerk or registrar of the court that granted the divorce or annulment. Once again, the fee for obtaining copies varies in each state and may also depend upon the number of pages in the document.

Write a letter to the court that granted the decree or judgment to inquire about the cost of obtaining a copy of the document. You'll need to give the names of the parties, the case number (if you know it), and the date and year the divorce or annulment was granted. Enclose a self-addressed, stamped envelope along with your payment.

✔ Complete a Personal Medication Record

Carrying with you at all times a record of the medications you are taking can be life-saving. If you should have a sudden illness, emergency responders and your family need to know promptly what medications you have been taking, any medical conditions for which you are receiving treatment, and any allergies you might have.

On the Personal Medication Record, list your prescription drugs as well as any over-the-counter drugs, vitamins, or herbal or dietary supplements. Also include the reason you are taking each medication along with the pharmacy and prescribing physician, if any. If you are not sure why you are taking a prescribed medication, ask your doctor. You can also list the form of the medication, such as a pill, liquid, patch or injection, and dosage, for example, how many milligrams are in each tablet. Note the frequency, too, such as "one pill at breakfast." In the last column, you can include any special directions, such as "with food."

Carry a copy with you all the time and share this information with your pharmacists. At each appointment, review the list with your doctors. Also make sure that a family member knows what medications you are taking. Your caregivers should keep a copy with them at all times, too.

✔ Organize tax files by year

Your past tax returns can be an invaluable source of information that your executor or personal representative may need to know. Your executor will be responsible for filing your income tax return for the year of your death. Your executor will also need to prepare any estate tax returns. Being able to readily locate recent returns and the supporting documentation for any schedules or itemized deductions can save your executor much time and frustration.

I keep each year's return and all the supporting documents in a portable file box, with separate folders for donations, bills, mortgage statements, and W-2 forms. An added benefit: Having these documents in one place also helps you prepare your next year's tax return.

✔ List all employers

By listing all your past employers, your executor will be able to quickly determine places to check about any benefits, pensions, retirement accounts, insurance benefits, or even unpaid leave that might be available for your heirs.

✔ Keep original documents that are valuable or irreplaceable in a safe deposit box

Use the Where to Find It Checklist starting on page 35 to list where you are keeping many of your records, lists, and documents. You can check off the items that are in your safe deposit box or note where you are storing other information, including copies of all the checklists in this book. Keep only the most important documents—not what you need to update frequently or readily access—in your safe deposit.

Note on the checklist where you've stored the documents: in your desk drawer, in a fireproof box in the den, or in the filing cabinet in the basement. You don't want to turn finding papers into a scavenger hunt.

Personal History Action Checklists

The checklists in Chapter 1 are set out in the following order:

- *Personal History*
- *Awards*
- *Biography*
- *Contacts*
- *Education*
- *Employment*
- *Memberships*
- *Personal Medication Record*
- *Pets*
- *Religion, Politics, and Hobbies*
- *Residences*
- *Where to Find It*
- *Personal History: Other*

Personal History

Name: _____

                      First   *Middle*   *Last*

Name at birth: _____

                      First   *Middle*   *Last*

Place of birth: _____

                      City   *State*   *Country*

Date of birth: _____

Date of adoption: _____

Legal name change: _____

                      First   *Middle*   *Last*

Legal name change date: _____

Legal name change court: _____

                           Court   *City*   *State*

****

Current address: _____

_____

How many years: _____

Phone: _____ Cell phone: _____

Email: _____ Fax: _____

****

Occupation or industry:_____

How many years: _____

****

Citizenship: _____

 ☐ By birth

 ☐ By naturalization

Naturalization date:_____

Naturalization place: _____

        City   *State*   *Country*

****

Military veteran:

 ☐ Yes

 ☐ No

Branch of service: _____

Dates of service: _____

Serial # (DD214): _____Rank: _____

Type of discharge: _____

****

Social Security #: _____

Passport #: _____ Expiration: _____

Country of issue: _____

Drivers license #: _____ Expiration: _____

State of issue: _____

****

I am registered to vote at Precinct:_____ County: _____ State: _____

Faith/Denomination: _____

Place of worship: _____

Address: _____

Pastor/Priest/Rabbi/Spiritual leader: _____

Phone:_____ Email: _____

****

My blood type: _____

****

Marital Status:

☐ Divorced

☐ Married

☐ Never married

☐ Widowed

First Spouse

Name of spouse at birth: _____

Date of birth: _____

Place of birth: _____

Date of marriage: _____

Date of divorce:_____

Date of death: _____

Spouse is buried at: _____

Cause of death: _____

Name at present: _____

Phone:_____ Email: _____

Address: _____

_____

Second Spouse

Name of spouse at birth: _____

Date of birth: _____

Place of birth: _____

Date of marriage: _____

Date of divorce:_____

Date of death: _____

Spouse is buried at: _____

Cause of death: _____

Name at present: _____

Phone:_____ Email: _____

Address: _____

_____

Third Spouse

Name of spouse at birth: _____

Date of birth:_____

Place of birth: _____

Date of marriage: _____

Date of divorce:_____

Date of death: _____

Spouse is buried at: _____

Cause of death: _____

Name at present: _____

Phone:_____ Email: _____

Address: _____

_____

Awards

I received the following academic awards and scholarships:

_____

_____

_____

_____

_____

_____

_____

_____

I received the following athletic awards and scholarships:

_____

_____

_____

_____

_____

_____

_____

_____

I received the following work-related awards and commendations:

_____

_____

_____

_____

_____

_____

_____

_____

Biography

These are the highlights to include in my biography:

_____

_____

_____

_____

_____

_____

_____

_____

_____

_____

_____

_____

_____

_____

_____

_____

_____

_____

_____

_____

_____

_____

_____

_____

_____

_____

_____

_____

_____

_____

Contacts

Advisers

Accountant: _____

Phone:_____ Email: _____

Website:_____

Address: _____

_____

Attorney: _____

Phone:_____ Email: _____

Website:_____

Address: _____

_____

Banker: _____

Phone:_____ Email: _____

Website:_____

Address: _____

_____

Executor: _____

Phone:_____ Email: _____

Website:_____

Address: _____

_____

Insurance agent: _____

Phone:_____ Email: _____

Website:_____

Address: _____

_____

Investment adviser: _____

Phone:_____ Email: _____

Website:_____

Address: _____

_____

Tax adviser:_____

Phone:_____ Email: _____

Website:_____

Address: _____

_____

Spiritual leader/Pastor/Priest: _____

Phone:_____ Email: _____

Website:_____

Address: _____

_____

Other: _____

Phone:_____ Email: _____

Website:_____

Address: _____

_____

Medical Professionals

Primary physician: _____

Phone:_____ Email: _____

Website:_____

Address: _____

_____

Specialty physician: _____

Phone: _____ Email: _____

Website: _____

Address: _____

_____

Specialty physician: _____

Phone: _____ Email: _____

Website: _____

Address: _____

_____

Dentist: _____

Phone: _____ Email: _____

Website: _____

Address: _____

_____

Other: _____

Phone: _____ Email: _____

Website: _____

Address: _____

_____

Service Providers

Children's babysitter: _____

Phone: _____ Email: _____

Website: _____

Address: _____

_____

Children's dentist: _____

Phone:_____ Email: _____

Website:_____

Address: _____

_____

Children's physician: _____

Phone:_____ Email: _____

Website:_____

Address: _____

_____

Children's school/Daycare:_____

Phone: _____ Email. _____

Website:_____

Address: _____

_____

Housekeeper:_____

Phone:_____ Email: _____

Website:_____

Address: _____

_____

Lawn service/Gardener: _____

Phone:_____ Email: _____

Website:_____

Address: _____

_____

Home health agency:_____

Phone:_____ Email: _____

Website:_____

Address: _____

_____

Home maintenance: _____

Phone:_____ Email: _____

Website:_____

Address: _____

_____

Pet's veterinarian: _____

Phone:_____ Email: _____

Website:_____

Address: _____

_____

Property manager:_____

Phone:_____ Email: _____

Website:_____

Address: _____

_____

Security system: _____

Phone:_____ Email: _____

Website:_____

Address: _____

_____

Education

I attended the following elementary or grade schools:

Name of school: _____

Location: _____

Grades attended:_____ Dates attended: _____

Name of school: _____

Location: _____

Grades attended:_____ Dates attended: _____

I attended the following middle schools, junior high schools, or high schools:

Name of school: _____

Location: _____

Grades attended:_____ Dates attended: _____

Name of school: _____

Location: _____

Grades attended:_____ Dates attended: _____

Name of school: _____

Location: _____

Grades attended:_____ Dates attended: _____

I attended the following preparatory schools:

Name of school: _____

Location: _____

Grades attended:_____ Dates attended: _____

Name of school: _____

Location: _____

Grades attended:_____ Dates attended: _____

I attended the following colleges or universities:

Name of school: _____

Location: _____

Degree/Certificate: _____

Dates attended/Graduated: _____

Name of school: _____

Location: _____

Degree/Certificate: _____

Dates attended/Graduated: _____

I attended the following additional schools and training programs:

Name of school: _____

Location: _____

Degree/Certificate: _____

Dates attended/Graduated: _____

I was involved in the following extracurricular activities (art, athletic, debate, drama, fraternity, music, school newspaper, sorority, etc.):

_____

_____

_____

_____

_____

_____

_____

_____

_____

_____

Employment

I am presently employed at the following company and job:

Employer: _____

Address: _____

Contact: _____

Type of work/Job title: _____

I worked at the following companies and jobs listed below:

Employer: _____

Address: _____

Contact: _____

Type of work/Job title: _____

Dates: _____

Employer: _____

Address: _____

Contact: _____

Type of work/Job title: _____

Dates: _____

Employer: _____

Address: _____

Contact: _____

Type of work/Job title: _____

Dates: _____

Employer: _____

Address: _____

Contact: _____

Type of work/Job title: _____

Dates: _____

Employer: _____

Address: _____

Contact: _____

Type of work/Job title: _____

Dates: _____

Employer: _____

Address: _____

Contact: _____

Type of work/Job title: _____

Dates: _____

Employer: _____

Address: _____

Contact: _____

Type of work/Job title: _____

Dates: _____

I retired on: _____ *(Date)*

These accomplishments and interesting projects concerning my employment may be of interest:

_____

_____

_____

_____

_____

_____

_____

_____

_____

_____

Memberships

I belong to the following organizations:

Membership organization: _____

Phone: _____ Website: _____

Address: _____

_____

Involvement: _____

Interesting facts: _____

_____

_____

Membership organization: _____

Phone: _____ Website: _____

Address: _____

_____

Involvement: _____

Interesting facts: _____

_____

_____

Membership organization: _____

Phone: _____ Website: _____

Address: _____

_____

Involvement: _____

Interesting facts: _____

_____

_____

Membership organization: _____

Phone: _____ Website: _____

Address: _____

_____

Involvement: _____

Interesting facts: _____

_____

_____

Membership organization: _____

Phone: _____ Website: _____

Address: _____

_____

Involvement: _____

Interesting facts: _____

_____

_____

I have the following season tickets:

Sports: _____

Phone: _____ Website: _____

Address: _____

_____

Seat numbers: _____

Theater: _____

Phone: _____ Website: _____

Address: _____

_____

Seat numbers: _____

Personal Medication Record

My Personal Information:

Name: _____

Date of birth: _____

Phone: _____

Emergency Contact:

Name: _____

Relationship: _____

Phone Number: _____

Primary Care Physician:

Name: _____

Phone: _____

Website: _____

Pharmacy/Drugstore:

Name: _____

Pharmacist: _____

Phone: _____

Website: _____

Other Physicians:

Name: _____

Specialty: _____

Phone: _____

Website: _____

Name: _____

Specialty: _____

Phone: _____

Website: _____

My Medical Conditions:

_____

_____

_____

_____

_____

_____

_____

_____

_____

_____

_____

My Allergies:

_____

_____

_____

_____

_____

_____

My Notes:

_____

_____

_____

_____

_____

_____

_____

_____

_____

_____

_____

_____

Medications

What	Reason	Form	Dosage	When	Notes

Be sure to include *all* prescription drugs, over-the-counter drugs, vitamins, and herbal or dietary supplements.

Pets

I own the following pets:

Pet name: _____

Type/Species/Coloring: _____

Birth date: _____ Ownership/Adoption date: _____

Instructions on food, water, care, exercise: _____

_____

_____

_____

Veterinarian: _____

Phone: _____ Website: _____

Address: _____

_____

Email: _____

Breeder: _____

Phone: _____ Website: _____

Address: _____

_____

Email: _____

Groomer: _____

Phone: _____ Website: _____

Address: _____

_____

Email: _____

Pet name: _____

Type/Species/Coloring: _____

Birth date: _____ Ownership/Adoption date: _____

Instructions on food, water, care, exercise: _____

_____

_____

_____

Veterinarian: _____

Phone: _____ Website: _____

Address: _____

_____

Email: _____

Breeder: _____

Phone: _____ Website: _____

Address: _____

_____

Email: _____

Groomer: _____

Phone: _____ Website: _____

Address: _____

_____

Email: _____

Pet name: _____

Type/Species/Coloring: _____

Birth date: _____ Ownership/Adoption date: _____

Instructions on food, water, care, exercise: _____

_____

_____

_____

Veterinarian: _____

Phone: _____ Website: _____

Address: _____

_____

Email: _____

Breeder: _____

Phone: _____ Website: _____

Address: _____

_____

Email: _____

Groomer: _____

Phone: _____ Website: _____

Address: _____

_____

Email: _____

Pet name: _____

Type/Species/Coloring: _____

Birth date: _____ Ownership/Adoption date: _____

Instructions on food, water, care, exercise: _____

_____

_____

_____

Veterinarian: _____

Phone: _____ Website: _____

Address: _____

_____

Email: _____

Breeder: _____

Phone: _____ Website: _____

Address: _____

_____

Email: _____

Groomer: _____

Phone: _____ Website: _____

Address: _____

_____

Email: _____

Pet name: _____

Type/Species/Coloring: _____

Birth date: _____ Ownership/Adoption date: _____

Instructions on food, water, care, exercise: _____

_____

_____

_____

Veterinarian: _____

Phone: _____ Website: _____

Address: _____

_____

Email: _____

Breeder: _____

Phone: _____ Website: _____

Address: _____

_____

Email: _____

Groomer: _____

Phone: _____ Website: _____

Address: _____

_____

Email: _____

(See page 245 describing my wishes for the further care and placement of my pets.)

Religion, Politics, and Hobbies

My religious activities and beliefs are as follows:

_____
_____
_____
_____
_____
_____
_____
_____
_____

My politics are as follows:

_____
_____
_____
_____
_____
_____
_____
_____
_____

My hobbies are as follows:

_____
_____
_____
_____
_____
_____
_____
_____
_____

Residences

I lived in the following cities and states at the addresses listed below:

Address: _____

City:_____ State:_____ Dates: _____

Address: _____

City:_____ State:_____ Dates: _____

Address: _____

City:_____ State:_____ Dates: _____

Address: _____

City:_____ State:_____ Dates: _____

Address: _____

City:_____ State:_____ Dates: _____

Address: _____

City:_____ State:_____ Dates: _____

Address: _____

City:_____ State:_____ Dates: _____

Address: _____

City:_____ State:_____ Dates: _____

Address: _____

City:_____ State:_____ Dates: _____

Address: _____

City:_____ State:_____ Dates: _____

Address: _____

City:_____ State:_____ Dates: _____

Address: _____

City:_____ State:_____ Dates: _____

Address: _____

City:_____ State:_____ Dates: _____

Address: _____

City:_____ State:_____ Dates: _____

Address: _____

City:_____ State:_____ Dates: _____

Address: _____

City:_____ State:_____ Dates: _____

Address: _____

City:_____ State:_____ Dates: _____

Address: _____

City:_____ State:_____ Dates: _____

Address: _____

City:_____ State:_____ Dates: _____

Where to Find It

It's important to let your family know where you have placed these items for safe keeping. If you are not sure where something is located, now might be a good time to locate it. If you don't know where it is, your family may have an even harder time finding it.

For each document or item, indicate where it is, such as in your safe deposit box, a fireproof box, a filing cabinet, or an electronic file, or with this book. Obviously, not everything needs to be, or even should be, stored in a safe deposit box; many items wouldn't even fit.

My safe deposit box is located at _____ (bank name), _____ (address), _____ (box number).

Record Type	Safe Deposit Box	Other Location
Personal History		
Adoption papers	☐	_____
Alimony settlement agreement	☐	_____
Animal care information	☐	_____
Annulment decrees or judgments	☐	_____
Appointment book or calendar	☐	_____
Athletic awards	☐	_____
Award certificates	☐	_____
Birth certificates	☐	_____
Caregiving information: Children	☐	_____
Caregiving information: Parents	☐	_____
Change of name certificates	☐	_____
Citizenship/naturalization	☐	_____

Record Type	Safe Deposit Box	Other Location
Civic awards	☐	_____
Cohabitation agreement	☐	_____
Digital photos	☐	_____
Divorce decrees or judgments	☐	_____
Durable power of attorney for finance	☐	_____
Durable power of attorney for health care	☐	_____
Dramatic awards	☐	_____
Drivers license	☐	_____
Educational awards	☐	_____
Educational certificates	☐	_____
Educational transcripts	☐	_____
Employment awards	☐	_____
Keys to post office box	☐	_____
Keys to residence	☐	_____
Keys to safe deposit box	☐	_____
Keys to vehicles	☐	_____
Keys to other real estate	☐	_____
Lock combinations	☐	_____
Membership awards	☐	_____
Membership certificates	☐	_____
Mental health power of attorney	☐	_____

Record Type	Safe Deposit Box	Other Location
Military awards	☐	_____
Military separation papers	☐	_____
Music/CDs catalog	☐	_____
Other awards	☐	_____
Passport	☐	_____
Passwords	☐	_____
Pet care	☐	_____
Photo albums	☐	_____
Postnuptial agreement	☐	_____
Prenuptial agreement	☐	_____
Property care information	☐	_____
Property settlement agreement	☐	_____
Qualified Domestic Relations Order (QDRO)	☐	_____
Security system information	☐	_____
Storage unit location	☐	_____
Tax returns and records	☐	_____
Timeshare records	☐	_____
Videos/movies catalog	☐	_____
Other	☐	_____
Other	☐	_____
Other	☐	_____

Record Type	Safe Deposit Box	Other Location
Family History		
Adoption papers: Children	☐	_____
Adoption papers: Pets	☐	_____
Birth certificates	☐	_____
Citizenship/naturalization papers	☐	_____
Family tree	☐	_____
Marriage certificates	☐	_____
Newspaper articles	☐	_____
Photo albums	☐	_____
Portraits	☐	_____
Other	☐	_____
Other	☐	_____
Other	☐	_____
Insurance Policies		
Annuities	☐	_____
Automobile	☐	_____
Boat	☐	_____
Homeowner	☐	_____
Life	☐	_____
Long-term care	☐	_____
Medical	☐	_____
Medicare card	☐	_____

Record Type	Safe Deposit Box	Other Location
Medicare Part D	☐	_____
Medicare supplemental	☐	_____
Pre-need funeral contract	☐	_____
Renters	☐	_____
Umbrella	☐	_____
Other	☐	_____
Other	☐	_____
Other	☐	_____
Benefits		
401(k) agreements	☐	_____
403(b) agreements	☐	_____
Disability agreements	☐	_____
IRA agreements/statements	☐	_____
Keogh plan agreements/statements	☐	_____
Medicare summary notices	☐	_____
Military separation papers	☐	_____
Pension agreements	☐	_____
SEP agreements/statements	☐	_____
Social Security benefit statement	☐	_____
Social Security card	☐	_____
Workers' compensation	☐	_____
Other	☐	_____

Record Type	Safe Deposit Box	Other Location
Other	☐	_____
Other	☐	_____
Banking and Savings		
Checking account statements	☐	_____
Credit union account statements	☐	_____
Savings account statements	☐	_____
Other	☐	_____
Other	☐	_____
Other	☐	_____
Investments		
Brokerage account statements	☐	_____
Certificates of deposit	☐	_____
Savings bonds	☐	_____
Other	☐	_____
Other	☐	_____
Other	☐	_____
Real Estate		
Cemetery deed	☐	_____
Deeds	☐	_____
Easements	☐	_____
Home improvement records	☐	_____

Record Type	Safe Deposit Box	Other Location
Land contracts	☐	_____
Leases	☐	_____
Mineral rights	☐	_____
Mortgages	☐	_____
Reverse mortgage	☐	_____
Tax records	☐	_____
Timeshare agreements	☐	_____
Other	☐	_____
Other	☐	_____
Other	☐	_____
Other Assets and Debts		
Business records	☐	_____
Computers	☐	_____
Copyrights	☐	_____
Collectibles	☐	_____
Credit card contracts	☐	_____
Jewelry appraisals	☐	_____
Jewelry inventory	☐	_____
Patents and trademarks	☐	_____
Rare books	☐	_____
Vehicles	☐	_____

Record Type	Safe Deposit Box	Other Location
Vehicles' certificates of title	☐	_____
Warranties	☐	_____
Websites	☐	_____
Other	☐	_____
Other	☐	_____
Other	☐	_____
Estate Planning		
Durable power of attorney	☐	_____
Letter of instruction	☐	_____
Trust agreement	☐	_____
Will and codicils	☐	_____
Other	☐	_____
Other	☐	_____
Other	☐	_____
Final Wishes		
Body bequeathal papers	☐	_____
Celebration of life prearrangements	☐	_____
Cemetery deed	☐	_____
Cremation prearrangement agreement	☐	_____
Ethical will/Legacy documents	☐	_____
Funeral prearrangement agreement	☐	_____

Record Type	Safe Deposit Box	Other Location
Health care directives	☐	_____
Legacy information	☐	_____
Letters to be sent	☐	_____
Living will	☐	_____
Mausoleum deed	☐	_____
Obituary	☐	_____
Pet continuing care	☐	_____
People to contact	☐	_____
Uniform organ donor card	☐	_____
Other	☐	_____
Other	☐	_____
Other	☐	_____

Personal History: Other

The following miscellaneous information about me may be of interest:

_____

_____

_____

_____

_____

_____

_____

_____

_____

_____

_____

_____

_____

_____

_____

_____

_____

_____

_____

_____

_____

_____

_____

_____

_____

_____

_____

_____

_____

CHAPTER 2
FAMILY HISTORY

The golden moments in the stream of life rush past us
and we see nothing but sand; the angels come to visit
us, and we only know them when they are gone.

—George Eliot

Information that you know about your parents and grandparents could easily be lost. With each passing generation, it becomes harder to track down when a distant relative settled in this country or where a favorite grandparent is buried. In this chapter, you can do a little digging to learn about your family while building a richer legacy for the next generation.

My To-Do Checklist

Done	Need to Do	
☐	☐	Take advantage of family gatherings or reunions to get help compiling family history information
☐	☐	Complete the Family Medical History Checklist
☐	☐	Complete the checklists for Chapter 2

Go through the checklists in Chapter 2 and fill in as many answers as you can. You may have many blanks when you finish. Make gathering the rest of the answers an enjoyable fact-finding adventure. Telephone, drop a note, or email your grandparent, parent, brother, sister, aunt, uncle, son, or daughter and gradually complete your personal history. As a bonus, you may even rekindle family ties.

In all the other chapters, the checklists are in alphabetical order, but in this chapter they are relatives, listed according to how they might inherit if you do not have a will. This is called intestate succession, which you'll learn more about in Chapter 9.

Checklists are provided for multiple spouses, children, and siblings. Please feel free to add more lines or to modify them to suit your needs. For example, if you are unmarried but have someone significant you would like to include, simply cross through *spouse* and replace it with the term you prefer to describe your relationship, such as *lifetime partner* or *special friend.*

✔ **Take advantage of family gatherings or reunions to get help compiling family history information**

You have space to write personal notes about your relatives. Use the space as you wish. For example, you can give a brief history, explain their beliefs or accomplishments, or share personal reminiscences. Here is a place to pass on those special moments you shared with a grandparent or the funny story about your brother when you were kids.

While you are searching out information about your relatives, this is a good time to note when and where they were born, as well as when they died and the cause of death. You can find this information on birth certificates and on death certificates. Census records, obituaries in newspapers, and online genealogical sites can also be helpful resources to track down missing information about your ancestors.

✔ **Complete the Family Medical History Checklist**

By completing the Family Medical History Checklist, you will be sharing information that may prove valuable in the diagnosis, early treatment, and, in some cases, prevention of certain hereditary medical conditions. You and your family can use this information to see if there are common illnesses or medical conditions in your family. This will help your family identify possible risks for certain diseases and ways to reduce or prevent those risks in the future.

You'll probably need to work with other family members in filling out the Family Medical History Checklist. Keep in mind that some family members may be unwilling to share this personal information. You will need to respect the privacy of anyone who is not comfortable revealing this information.

Family History Action Checklists

The checklists in Chapter 2 are set out in the following order:

- *Children*
- *Parents*
- *Brothers and Sisters*
- *Grandparents*
- *Aunts, Uncles, and Cousins*
- *Stepparents*
- *Stepbrothers and Stepsisters*
- *Stepgrandparents*
- *Family Medical History*
- *Family History: Other*

Children

Name at present: _____

Phone: _____ Email: _____

Address: _____

_____

Favorite memories:

_____

_____

_____

Name at birth: _____

Place of birth: _____

              City   County   State   Country

Child is buried at: _____

Cause of death: _____

    ☐ Child has never been married.

    ☐ Child is currently married.

    ☐ Child has been married _____ times.

	Name of Spouse	Date of Marriage	Date of Divorce	Date of Death
# 1				
# 2				
# 3				

    ☐ Child has not had any children.

    ☐ Child has _____ born children.

    ☐ Child has _____ adopted children.

	Name of Child at Birth	Current Name of Child	Date of Birth	Date of Death
# 1				
# 2				
# 3				
# 4				
# 5				
# 6				

****

Name at present: _____

Phone: _____ Email: _____

Address: _____

_____

Favorite memories:

_____

_____

_____

Name at birth: _____

Place of birth: _____

            City   *County*   *State*   *Country*

Child is buried at: _____

Cause of death: _____

- ☐ Child has never been married.
- ☐ Child is currently married.
- ☐ Child has been married _____ times.

	Name of Spouse	Date of Marriage	Date of Divorce	Date of Death
# 1				
# 2				
# 3				

☐   Child has not had any children.

☐   Child has _____ born children.

☐   Child has _____ adopted children.

	Name of Child at Birth	Current Name of Child	Date of Birth	Date of Death
# 1				
# 2				
# 3				
# 4				
# 5				
# 6				

****

Name at present: _____

Phone: _____ Email: _____

Address: _____

_____

Favorite memories:

_____

_____

_____

Name at birth: _____

Place of birth: _____

                               City   *County*   *State*   *Country*

Child is buried at: _____

Cause of death: _____

- ☐ Child has never been married.
- ☐ Child is currently married.
- ☐ Child has been married _____ times.

	Name of Spouse	Date of Marriage	Date of Divorce	Date of Death
# 1				
# 2				
# 3				

- ☐ Child has not had any children.
- ☐ Child has _____ born children.
- ☐ Child has _____ adopted children.

	Name of Child at Birth	Current Name of Child	Date of Birth	Date of Death
# 1				
# 2				
# 3				
# 4				

# 5				
# 6				

****

Name at present: _____

Phone: _____ Email:_____

Address: _____

_____

Favorite memories:

_____

_____

_____

Name at birth: _____

Place of birth: _____

                    City   Count   State   Country

Child is buried at: _____

Cause of death: _____

☐ Child has never been married.

☐ Child is currently married.

☐ Child has been married _____ times.

	Name of Spouse	Date of Marriage	Date of Divorce	Date of Death
# 1				
# 2				
# 3				

☐ Child has not had any children.

☐ Child has _____ born children.

☐ Child has _____ adopted children.

	Name of Child at Birth	Current Name of Child	Date of Birth	Date of Death
# 1				
# 2				
# 3				
# 4				
# 5				
# 6				

Parents

Name: _____

☐ Father   ☐ Mother

Phone: _____ Email: _____

Address: _____

_____

Date of birth: _____ Place of birth: _____

Date of death: _____ Cause of death: _____

Favorite memories:

_____

_____

_____

_____

_____

_____

_____

_____

_____

_____

_____

_____

_____

_____

_____

_____

_____

_____

_____

_____

Name: _____

☐ Father   ☐ Mother

Phone: _____ Email: _____

Address: _____

_____

Date of birth: _____ Place of birth: _____

Date of death: _____ Cause of death: _____

Favorite memories:

_____

_____

_____

_____

_____

_____

_____

_____

_____

_____

_____

_____

_____

_____

_____

_____

_____

_____

_____

_____

_____

_____

_____

_____

_____

_____

Brothers and Sisters

Name at present: _____

Phone: _____ Email:_____

Address: _____

_____

How this person is related to me: _____

Favorite memories:

_____

_____

_____

_____

Date of birth: _____

Place of birth: _____

| | City | County | State | Country |

Date of death: _____ Cause of death:_____

Sibling is buried at: _____

☐ Sibling has never been married.

☐ Sibling is currently married.

☐ Sibling has been married _____ times.

	Name of Spouse	Date of Marriage	Date of Divorce	Date of Death
# 1				
# 2				
# 3				

☐ Sibling has not had any children.

☐ Sibling has _____ born children..

☐ Sibling has _____ adopted children.

	Name of Child at Birth	Current Name of Child	Date of Birth	Date of Death
# 1				
# 2				
# 3				
# 4				
# 5				
# 6				

****

Name at present: _____

Phone: _____ Email: _____

Address: _____

_____

How this person is related to me: _____

Favorite memories:

_____

_____

_____

Date of birth: _____

Place of birth: _____

                                City   *County*   *State*   *Country*

Date of death: _____ Cause of death:_____

Sibling is buried at: _____

☐ Sibling has never been married.

☐ Sibling is currently married.

☐ Sibling has been married _____ times.

	Name of Spouse	Date of Marriage	Date of Divorce	Date of Death
# 1				
# 2				
# 3				

☐ Sibling has not had any children.

☐ Sibling has _____ born children.

☐ Sibling has _____ adopted children.

	Name of Child at Birth	Current Name of Child	Date of Birth	Date of Death
# 1				
# 2				
# 3				
# 4				
# 5				
# 6				

****

Name at present: _____

Phone: _____ Email: _____

Address: _____

_____

How this person is related to me: _____

Favorite memories:

_____

_____

_____

_____

Date of birth: _____

Place of birth: _____

                                City   *County*   *State*   *Country*

Date of death: _____ Cause of death: _____

Sibling is buried at: _____

☐ Sibling has never been married.

☐ Sibling is currently married.

☐ Sibling has been married _____ times.

	Name of Spouse	Date of Marriage	Date of Divorce	Date of Death
# 1				
# 2				
# 3				

☐ Sibling has not had any children.

☐ Sibling has _____ born children.

☐ Sibling has _____ adopted children.

	Name of Child at Birth	Current Name of Child	Date of Birth	Date of Death
# 1				
# 2				
# 3				

# 4				
# 5				
# 6				

****

Name at present: _____

Phone: _____ Email: _____

Address: _____

_____

How this person is related to me: _____

Favorite memories:

_____

_____

_____

Date of birth: _____

Place of birth: _____

City   County   State   Country

Date of death: _____ Cause of death: _____

Sibling is buried at: _____

☐   Sibling has never been married.

☐   Sibling is currently married.

☐   Sibling has been married _____ times.

	Name of Spouse	Date of Marriage	Date of Divorce	Date of Death
# 1				
# 2				
# 3				

☐ Sibling has not had any children.

☐ Sibling has _____ born children.

☐ Sibling has _____ adopted children.

	Name of Child at Birth	Current Name of Child	Date of Birth	Date of Death
# 1				
# 2				
# 3				
# 4				
# 5				
# 6				

****

Name at present: _____

Phone: _____ Email: _____

Address: _____

_____

How this person is related to me: _____

Favorite memories:

_____

_____

_____

_____

Date of birth: _____

Place of birth: _____

       City   *County*   *State*   *Country*

Date of death: _____ Cause of death:_____

Sibling is buried at _____

    ☐ Sibling has never been married.

    ☐ Sibling is currently married.

    ☐ Sibling has been married _____ times.

	Name of Spouse	Date of Marriage	Date of Divorce	Date of Death
# 1				
# 2				
# 3				

    ☐ Sibling has not had any children.

    ☐ Sibling has _____ born children.

    ☐ Sibling has _____ adopted children.

	Name of Child at Birth	Current Name of Child	Date of Birth	Date of Death
# 1				
# 2				
# 3				
# 4				
# 5				
# 6				

****

Name at present: _____

Phone: _____ Email: _____

Address: _____

_____

How this person is related to me: _____

Favorite memories:

_____

_____

_____

_____

Date of birth: _____

Place of birth: _____

                         City   *County*   *State*   *Country*

Date of death: _____ Cause of death: _____

Sibling is buried at: _____

☐ Sibling has never been married.

☐ Sibling is currently married.

☐ Sibling has been married _____ times.

	Name of Spouse	Date of Marriage	Date of Divorce	Date of Death
# 1				
# 2				
# 3				

☐ Sibling has not had any children.

☐ Sibling has _____ born children.

☐ Sibling has _____ adopted children.

	Name of Child at Birth	Current Name of Child	Date of Birth	Date of Death
# 1				
# 2				
# 3				
# 4				
# 5				
# 6				

Grandparents

Name: _____

☐ Paternal grandfather ☐ Paternal grandmother

☐ Maternal grandfather ☐ Maternal grandmother

Phone: _____ Email: _____

Address: _____

_____

Date of birth: _____ Place of birth: _____

Date of death: _____ Cause of death: _____

Favorite memories:

_____

_____

_____

_____

_____

Name: _____

☐ Paternal grandfather ☐ Paternal grandmother

☐ Maternal grandfather ☐ Maternal grandmother

Phone: _____ Email: _____

Address: _____

_____

Date of birth: _____ Place of birth: _____

Date of death: _____ Cause of death: _____

Favorite memories:

_____

_____

_____

_____

_____

Name: _____

☐ Paternal grandfather   ☐ Paternal grandmother

☐ Maternal grandfather   ☐ Maternal grandmother

Phone: _____ Email: _____

Address: _____

_____

Date of birth: _____ Place of birth: _____

Date of death: _____ Cause of death: _____

Favorite memories:

_____

_____

_____

_____

_____

Name: _____

☐ Paternal grandfather   ☐ Paternal grandmother

☐ Maternal grandfather   ☐ Maternal grandmother

Phone: _____ Email: _____

Address: _____

_____

Date of birth: _____ Place of birth: _____

Date of death: _____ Cause of death: _____

Favorite memories:

_____

_____

_____

_____

_____

Aunts, Uncles, and Cousins

Name: _____

How this person is related to me: _____

Phone: _____ Email: _____

Address: _____

_____

Date of birth: _____ Place of birth: _____

Date of death: _____ Cause of death: _____

Favorite memories:

_____

_____

_____

_____

_____

_____

Name: _____

How this person is related to me: _____

Phone: _____ Email: _____

Address: _____

_____

Date of birth: _____ Place of birth: _____

Date of death: _____ Cause of death: _____

Favorite memories:

_____

_____

_____

_____

_____

_____

Name: _____

How this person is related to me: _____

Phone: _____ Email: _____

Address: _____

_____

Date of birth: _____ Place of birth: _____

Date of death: _____ Cause of death: _____

Favorite memories:

_____

_____

_____

_____

_____

_____

Name: _____

How this person is related to me: _____

Phone: _____ Email: _____

Address: _____

_____

Date of birth: _____ Place of birth: _____

Date of death: _____ Cause of death: _____

Favorite memories:

_____

_____

_____

_____

_____

_____

© American Bar Association

Name: _____

How this person is related to me: _____

Phone: _____ Email: _____

Address: _____

_____

Date of birth: _____ Place of birth: _____

Date of death: _____ Cause of death: _____

Favorite memories:

_____

_____

_____

_____

_____

_____

Name: _____

How this person is related to me: _____

Phone: _____ Email: _____

Address: _____

_____

Date of birth: _____ Place of birth: _____

Date of death: _____ Cause of death: _____

Favorite memories:

_____

_____

_____

_____

_____

_____

Name: _____

How this person is related to me: _____

Phone: _____ Email: _____

Address: _____

_____

Date of birth: _____ Place of birth: _____

Date of death: _____ Cause of death: _____

Favorite memories:

_____

_____

_____

_____

_____

_____

Name: _____

How this person is related to me: _____

Phone: _____ Email: _____

Address: _____

_____

Date of birth: _____ Place of birth: _____

Date of death: _____ Cause of death: _____

Favorite memories:

_____

_____

_____

_____

_____

_____

Stepparents

Name: _____

☐ Stepfather   ☐ Stepmother

Phone: _____ Email: _____

Address: _____

_____

Date of birth: _____ Place of birth: _____

Date of death: _____ Cause of death: _____

Favorite memories:

_____

_____

_____

_____

_____

_____

Name: _____

☐ Stepfather   ☐ Stepmother

Phone: _____ Email: _____

Address: _____

_____

Date of birth: _____ Place of birth: _____

Date of death: _____ Cause of death: _____

Favorite memories:

_____

_____

_____

_____

_____

_____

Stepbrothers and Stepsisters

Name: _____

☐ Stepbrother   ☐ Stepsister

Phone: _____ Email: _____

Address: _____

_____

Date of birth: _____ Place of birth: _____

Date of death: _____ Cause of death: _____

Favorite memories:

_____

_____

_____

_____

_____

_____

Name: _____

☐ Stepfather   ☐ Stepmother

Phone: _____ Email: _____

Address: _____

_____

Date of birth: _____ Place of birth: _____

Date of death: _____ Cause of death: _____

Favorite memories:

_____

_____

_____

_____

_____

_____

Name: _____

☐ Stepbrother   ☐ Stepsister

Phone: _____ Email: _____

Address: _____

_____

Date of birth: _____ Place of birth: _____

Date of death: _____ Cause of death: _____

Favorite memories:

_____

_____

_____

_____

_____

Name: _____

☐ Stepfather   ☐ Stepmother

Phone: _____ Email: _____

Address: _____

_____

Date of birth: _____ Place of birth: _____

Date of death: _____ Cause of death: _____

Favorite memories:

_____

_____

_____

_____

_____

Stepgrandparents

Name: _____

☐ Paternal stepgrandfather   ☐ Paternal stepgrandmother

☐ Maternal stepgrandfather   ☐ Maternal stepgrandmother

Phone: _____ Email: _____

Address: _____

_____

Date of birth: _____ Place of birth: _____

Date of death: _____ Cause of death: _____

Favorite memories:

_____

_____

_____

_____

_____

Name: _____

☐ Paternal stepgrandfather   ☐ Paternal stepgrandmother

☐ Maternal stepgrandfather   ☐ Maternal stepgrandmother

Phone: _____ Email: _____

Address: _____

_____

Date of birth: _____ Place of birth: _____

Date of death: _____ Cause of death: _____

Favorite memories:

_____

_____

_____

_____

_____

Name: _____

☐ Paternal stepgrandfather   ☐ Paternal stepgrandmother

☐ Maternal stepgrandfather   ☐ Maternal stepgrandmother

Phone: _____ Email: _____

Address: _____

_____

Date of birth: _____ Place of birth: _____

Date of death: _____ Cause of death: _____

Favorite memories:

_____

_____

_____

_____

_____

Name: _____

☐ Paternal stepgrandfather   ☐ Paternal stepgrandmother

☐ Maternal stepgrandfather   ☐ Maternal stepgrandmother

Phone: _____ Email: _____

Address: _____

_____

Date of birth: _____ Place of birth: _____

Date of death: _____ Cause of death: _____

Favorite memories:

_____

_____

_____

_____

_____

Family Medical History

The following lists my family medical history. I or any of my blood relatives (including parents, grandparents, sisters, brothers, uncles, aunts, and children) have had the following:

Yes   **Who**

- ☐ Alcoholism   _____
- ☐ Allergies   _____
- ☐ Alzheimer's disease   _____
- ☐ Arthritis   _____
- ☐ Asthma   _____
- ☐ Birth defects   _____
- ☐ Blood disorder   _____
- ☐ Cancer   _____
- ☐ Chromosomal disorder   _____
- ☐ Cystic fibrosis   _____
- ☐ Diabetes   _____
- ☐ Dementia   _____
- ☐ Eczema   _____
- ☐ Endometriosis   _____
- ☐ Epilepsy   _____
- ☐ Gallbladder problems   _____
- ☐ Gastrointestinal disorders   _____
- ☐ Glaucoma   _____
- ☐ Gout   _____
- ☐ Hay fever   _____
- ☐ Hearing loss   _____
- ☐ Heart disease   _____
- ☐ High blood pressure   _____
- ☐ High cholesterol   _____
- ☐ Infertility   _____
- ☐ Inflammatory bowel disease   _____

- ☐ Intellectual disabilities   _____
- ☐ Kidney disease   _____
- ☐ Learning disabilities   _____
- ☐ Lung disease   _____
- ☐ Lymphoma   _____
- ☐ Mental disorder   _____
- ☐ Mental retardation   _____
- ☐ Miscarriage, stillbirth   _____
- ☐ Muscular dystrophy   _____
- ☐ Neurological disorders   _____
- ☐ Osteoporosis   _____
- ☐ Psoriasis   _____
- ☐ Sickle cell disease   _____
- ☐ Skin cancer: basal cell   _____
- ☐ Skin cancer: melanoma   _____
- ☐ Skin cancer: squamous cell   _____
- ☐ Stomach disorders   _____
- ☐ Stroke   _____
- ☐ Thyroid disorder   _____
- ☐ Ulcers   _____
- ☐ Vision impairment   _____
- ☐ Other   _____
- ☐ Other   _____

Notes about my family's medical history:

_____

_____

_____

_____

_____

_____

Family History: Other

The following miscellaneous information about my family history may be of interest:

_____

_____

_____

_____

_____

_____

_____

_____

_____

_____

_____

_____

_____

_____

_____

_____

_____

_____

_____

_____

_____

_____

_____

_____

_____

_____

_____

_____

_____

CHAPTER 3
INSURANCE

If you can keep your head when all about you
Are loving theirs and blaming it on you...
If you can meet with Triumph and Disaster
And threat those two imposters the same...
Yours is the Earth and everything that's in it,
And—which is more—you'll be a Man, my son!

—Rudyard Kipling

Insurance offers a way to spread the risk of financial loss among many people. The payment of annual premiums protects the insured (to the limits of the policy) against losses from fire, theft, accident, or liability, depending on the type of insurance purchased. Any loss is shared by all of those insured, saving the individual from financial disaster. The group, in other words, absorbs the individual's unexpected losses.

If something happens to you—death, an accident, a stroke, or other event that prevents you from continuing to conduct your own business affairs—your loved ones may have to file insurance claims, cancel certain policies, or obtain new ones in order to protect your property. To be able to take advantage of the insurance that you have obtained to protect your family and property, your family needs to know about all your insurance policies. An amazing number of insurance proceeds goes unclaimed because the policyholder's family or heirs were never told about them.

This chapter also gives you an opportunity to make sure you do have the insurance coverage that you need. To that end, you'll find overviews of the types of insurance available. Use the checklists in this chapter so your family has a record of your various policies with the names and addresses of the agents and companies.

My To-Do Checklist

Done   Need to Do

Done	Need to Do	
☐	☐	Review the terms of all insurance policies
☐	☐	Locate all insurance policies
☐	☐	Update the beneficiaries you have listed on your policies
☐	☐	Annually review your health, disability, Medicare, and long-term care insurance options
☐	☐	Keep vehicle insurance current
☐	☐	Review homeowners and renters insurance coverage
☐	☐	Complete the checklists for Chapter 3

The following descriptions are not a detailed breakdown of the many types of insurance options available. They should, however, give you some information about the most widely used types of insurance coverage to help you organize your own policies.

✔ Review the terms of all insurance policies

Annuity

Annuities are a type of insurance that are typically designed to provide a stream of income. As with other types of insurance, there are many types of annuities. They may be fixed, variable, or indexed, with immediate or deferred payments. Typically, money invested in the annuity grows tax-deferred, with payouts being taxed when received as return of principal and ordinary income.

You can have many options with annuities: how your money is invested within the annuity, at what point your annuity begins to make payments, and for how long and to whom payments will be made. Payouts may be made for a fixed number of years, or during your lifetime, or for the lifetime of a spouse or other beneficiary. You can also obtain, at additional cost, specific benefits, such as a guaranteed minimum death benefit or a guaranteed minimum withdrawal benefit. A guaranteed minimum death benefit, or GMDB rider, means that your beneficiaries or your estate will receive a set amount as defined in the contract if you die before the annuity begins paying benefits. A guaranteed minimum withdrawal benefit, or GMWB, means that while you are alive you will receive a fixed percentage of your investment each year. Be certain you understand the terms of any annuity you have and periodically review your annuity contract to confirm that it continues to fit your needs.

Life Insurance

Life insurance is primarily intended to ease the financial loss to a beneficiary that results from the policyholder's death. Although death comes to everyone and cannot be considered unexpected in the long run, it can certainly be unexpected when it occurs. Life insurance is a way to make sure that your family has cash to pay for your final expenses, such as for your funeral or the expenses of your final illness. An insurance policy could also provide cash for any estate taxes or unpaid debts as well as financial support to your spouse or dependent children after your death.

Today's life insurance market has multiple options for you to choose from including how much coverage you purchase, the size of the premiums, how the policy is invested, any guarantees on returns, and how and when the policy proceeds are paid out to your beneficiaries. Before purchasing any policy, you need to be certain you understand all of the options and the risks involved. This money may be paid in a lump sum, in a monthly sum for the life of another individual, in monthly sums over a certain length of time, or in some other manner spelled out by the terms of your policy. Regardless of what payment method you select, the amount your beneficiary will receive is set out in the policy. The amount may even pay double if your death is caused by accident—a so-called *double indemnity* policy. Do your homework to compare your options with multiple insurance companies. Also seek competent advice on any tax consequences to you and your estate that the various options can have.

A widely purchased form of life insurance is *whole life insurance*. This type of insurance pays a sum of money (the "face value") to your beneficiary at the time of your death. You have to pay a premium each year to keep the insurance in force. The amount of the premium is determined by your age at the time you purchased the policy. The younger you are, the smaller the premium on the policy. Variations in the method of payment for whole life insurance are available. For example, you might obtain a policy that requires annual premiums for twenty years. At the expiration of the 20-year period, the policy continues in effect for the balance of your life, but you do not have to continue paying the premiums. It is even possible for you to purchase a policy by making one large initial premium payment. Regardless of how you pay for the policy, whole life insurance provides coverage for the rest of your life (as long as you have paid all the required premiums).

Universal life, variable whole life, and variable universal life are different types of permanent life insurance in which you have the option to vary (within the terms of the contract) the amount you pay in premiums from year to year and how your policy's cash reserves grow. Typically the cash value reserves held by the insurance company are invested in stocks, bonds, or mutual funds. You, as the policyholder, are able to select the investment from a menu offered by the insurance company. Some policies have guaranteed minimum returns on the investment; others allow you to borrow against the cash value during your life. How much your beneficiary would receive at your death varies based on many factors, including the terms of the policy, the amounts paid in premiums, and the investment success of the insurance company.

Term insurance, on the other hand, provides insurance coverage only for a specified length of time. You might purchase a policy that provides coverage for five years, ten years, or twenty years. The annual premium for term insurance is substantially less than the annual premium for whole life insurance. The cost of purchasing the same amount of coverage gradually increases with the age of the purchaser. Many term life insurance contracts provide that the policy may be renewed at the end of the term without providing further proof of insurability. The premium for the renewed term will most likely be higher than for the original term because you would be older. Other term policies provide that they may be converted, within a certain period, into a permanent type of life insurance without proof of insurability. Once again, the premium would be adjusted.

✔ Locate all insurance policies

Regardless of the type of life insurance you hold, it is important that your life insurance policies be readily available at death, that they be kept in a safe place, and that your heirs know where they are located. Some companies may require that your heirs hand over your original life insurance policies before they can collect any proceeds.

Many employers provide life insurance for their employees, and partnerships often fund buy-sell agreements with life insurance. Be sure to include information about work-related insurance in the checklists in this chapter. You don't want your heirs to overlook any policies.

✔ Update the beneficiaries you have listed on your policies

Now is a good time to review each policy to make sure you have properly listed the names of those you want to receive the policy proceeds. You want to keep your list of beneficiaries up to date. Circumstances may have changed since you initially named the beneficiaries on your policies. For example, you probably don't want to have a former spouse as a beneficiary (unless you are required to maintain a policy under a divorce decree). Your family may have changed with marriages, divorces, births of children and grandchildren, and deaths. A beneficiary you named several years ago may now be deceased.

You can name one person, your estate, or multiple people as your beneficiaries. It's a good idea to name successor or secondary beneficiaries in case a primary beneficiary dies before you do. If you want to name more than one beneficiary, you should indicate the percentage that each is to receive. For example, you could name your spouse as the primary beneficiary to receive 100 percent of the policy and name your three children as secondary beneficiaries, with each receiving 33 percent if your spouse dies before you do.

✔ **Annually review your health, disability, Medicare, and long-term care insurance options**

Health Insurance

Health insurance provides a means to pay doctor, hospital, and other medical expenses if you become sick or are in an accident. Most people get health insurance as an employee benefit where they work. Some people can continue to get health coverage through their former employer's health plan after they retire. Employers don't have to provide *retiree health insurance* and they can cut or eliminate those benefits. Before you retire, or if you are retired, be sure you know what health benefits are available to you. Get this information from your employer's benefit coordinator. Typically, with group health insurance you have an opportunity each year to modify your coverage. If you don't have health insurance through your employer or union, you can obtain coverage through the Health Insurance Marketplace in your state.

Many different types of accident and illness insurance policies exist. Some are very limited in scope and pay out only if you develop a specific type of illness, such as cancer. Other policies, however, provide very broad coverage, though each has its limitations. Before purchasing any type of health insurance, be certain you understand what is and is not covered.

Medical expense reimbursement policies range from a policy that pays a fixed amount for each day you are hospitalized to health insurance policies that cover almost every medical expense that the policyholder could incur. Because the coverage varies to such a great extent, the cost of medical and accident coverage varies greatly. Be sure to review what coverage you have now and comparison shop for different coverage if your health, employment, or retirement circumstances have changed.

Disability insurance is intended to provide you and your family with financial stability if you should not be able to work because of an accident, injury, or illness. Some employers, unions, and professional associations provide disability insurance for their employees or members. Policies can vary in the amount of your income that would be replaced, how long you can receive the payments, and what types of disabilities you need to have before you can receive the benefits.

✔ **Keep vehicle insurance current**

If you own a motor vehicle—car, truck, motorcycle, motorboat, snowmobile, or other recreational vehicle—you probably have vehicle insurance. In fact, many states require all drivers to be insured for liability to other persons for damages resulting from an accident. Regardless of the law in your particular state, it makes good sense to insure yourself against the claims by others and against any expenses that you might have if you have a collision or fire or your vehicle is stolen.

✔ **Review homeowners and renters insurance coverage**

Originally, fire insurance was about the only type of insurance that homeowners could obtain on their residence. Now you can get insurance to protect against windstorm, hail, flood, explosion, riot, smoke damage, and more. Insurance is also available for the contents of your home, as well as your garage or any outbuildings.

Today, most homeowners purchase a homeowners policy that combines fire and extended insurance coverage that also includes protection for your personal property, additional living expenses if you can't live in your home because of damage, and comprehensive personal liability coverage. This personal liability coverage would make medical payments to guests who get injured in your home and pay for some damage to the property of others. Rather than having to purchase separate policies to cover each of these various risks, the homeowners policy combines them into one policy. Similar types of policies are available to condominium owners and renters that cover your personal property due to damage to the unit. You can also add *riders* to your policy to fit specific needs, or to insure special items such as antiques or jewelry.

Other Insurance

Many insurance companies offer additional insurance liability protection through an *umbrella policy,* which provides insurance coverage in excess of your regular automobile, personal liability, and other liability coverage. It is usually sold in multiples of $1 million and can be a low-cost method of buying substantial protection.

Insurance Action Checklists

The checklists in Chapter 3 are set out in the following order:

- *Annuity*
- *Health Insurance: Disability, Medicare, and Long-Term Care*
- *Homeowners and Renters Insurance*
- *Life Insurance*
- *Umbrella Insurance Policy*
- *Vehicle Insurance*
- *Insurance: Other*

Annuity

☐   I do not have an annuity.

☐   I have an annuity with the following policies and companies:

Insurance company: _____

Agent: _____

Phone: _____ Fax: _____

Address: _____

_____

Email: _____ Website: _____

Policy #: _____

Terms: _____

Beneficiary/beneficiaries: _____

Insurance company: _____

Agent: _____

Phone: _____ Fax: _____

Address: _____

_____

Email: _____ Website: _____

Policy #: _____

Terms: _____

Beneficiary/beneficiaries: _____

Insurance company: _____

Agent: _____

Phone: _____ Fax: _____

Address: _____

_____

Email: _____ Website: _____

Policy #: _____

Terms: _____

Beneficiary/beneficiaries: _____

Health Insurance: Disability, Medicare, and Long-Term Care

- ☐ I do not carry health insurance.
- ☐ I carry health insurance with the following policies and companies:
    - ☐ Dental
    - ☐ Disability
    - ☐ Hospitalization
    - ☐ Long-term care
    - ☐ Major medical
    - ☐ Medicare
    - ☐ Medicare Advantage
    - ☐ Medicare Part D Prescription Insurance (Medigap)
    - ☐ Medicare Supplemental Drug Insurance
    - ☐ Surgical
    - ☐ Travel accidental death
    - ☐ Vision
    - ☐ Other
- ☐ I have health insurance with the following companies

Insurance company: _____

Type of policy: _____

Policy #: _____

Group #: _____

Policy premium due date: _____

Agent: _____

Phone: _____ Fax: _____

Address: _____

_____

Email: _____ Website: _____

Insurance company: _____

Type of policy: _____

Policy #: _____

Group #: _____

Policy premium due date: _____

Agent: _____

Phone: _____ Fax: _____

Address: _____

_____

Email: _____ Website: _____

Insurance company: _____

Type of policy: _____

Policy #: _____

Group #: _____

Policy premium due date: _____

Agent: _____

Phone: _____ Fax: _____

Address: _____

_____

Email: _____ Website: _____

Insurance company: _____

Type of policy: _____

Policy #: _____

Group #: _____

Policy premium due date: _____

Agent: _____

Phone: _____ Fax: _____

Address: _____

_____

Email: _____ Website: _____

Insurance company: _____

Type of policy: _____

Policy #: _____

Group #: _____

Policy premium due date: _____

Agent: _____

Phone: _____ Fax: _____

Address: _____

_____

Email: _____ Website: _____

Insurance company: _____

Type of policy: _____

Policy #: _____

Group #: _____

Policy premium due date: _____

Agent: _____

Phone: _____ Fax: _____

Address: _____

_____

Email: _____ Website: _____

Insurance company: _____

Type of policy: _____

Policy #: _____

Group #: _____

Policy premium due date: _____

Agent: _____

Phone: _____ Fax: _____

Address: _____

_____

Email: _____ Website: _____

Homeowners and Renters Insurance

☐ I do not carry homeowners or residence insurance.

☐ I carry homeowners, renters, condominium, or second residence insurance policies with the following companies:

Insurance company: _____

Policy #: _____

Agent: _____

Phone: _____ Fax: _____

Address: _____

_____

Email: _____ Website: _____

Description of coverage:

_____

_____

Insurance company: _____

Policy #: _____

Agent: _____

Phone: _____ Fax: _____

Address: _____

_____

Email: _____ Website: _____

Description of coverage:

_____

_____

Life Insurance

☐   I do not carry life insurance.

☐   I carry life insurance with the following companies:

Insurance company: _____

Policy #: _____

Face amount: _____

Beneficiary/beneficiaries: _____

Agent: _____

Phone: _____ Fax: _____

Address: _____

_____

Email: _____ Website: _____

Insurance company: _____

Policy #: _____

Face amount: _____

Beneficiary/beneficiaries: _____

Agent: _____

Phone: _____ Fax: _____

Address: _____

_____

Email: _____ Website: _____

Umbrella Insurance Policy

☐   I do not carry an umbrella insurance policy.

☐   I have an umbrella insurance policy with the following companies:

Insurance company: _____

Policy #: _____

Group #: _____

Type of policy: _____

Policy premium due date: _____

Agent: _____

Phone: _____ Fax: _____

Address: _____

_____

Email: _____ Website: _____

Insurance company: _____

Policy #: _____

Group #: _____

Type of policy: _____

Policy premium due date: _____

Agent: _____

Phone: _____ Fax: _____

Address: _____

_____

Email: _____ Website: _____

Vehicle Insurance

☐ I do not carry vehicle insurance.

☐ I carry vehicle insurance on the following vehicles, including cars, airplanes, boats, motorcycles, and snowmobiles with the following companies:

Vehicle: _____

Year purchased:_____ Purchase price:_____

Insurance company: _____

Agent: _____

Phone: _____ Fax: _____

Address: _____

_____

Email: _____ Website: _____

Policy #: _____

Vehicle: _____

Year purchased:_____ Purchase price:_____

Insurance company: _____

Agent: _____

Phone: _____ Fax: _____

Address: _____

_____

Email: _____ Website: _____

Policy #: _____

Vehicle: _____

Year purchased:_____ Purchase price:_____

Insurance company: _____

Agent: _____

Phone: _____ Fax: _____

Address: _____

_____

Email: _____ Website: _____

Policy #: _____

Vehicle: _____

Year purchased:_____ Purchase price:_____

Insurance company: _____

Agent: _____

Phone: _____ Fax: _____

Address: _____

_____

Email: _____ Website: _____

Policy #: _____

Vehicle: _____

Year purchased:_____ Purchase price:_____

Insurance company: _____

Agent: _____

Phone: _____ Fax: _____

Address: _____

_____

Email: _____ Website: _____

Policy #: _____

Vehicle: _____

Year purchased:_____ Purchase price:_____

Insurance company: _____

Agent: _____

Phone: _____ Fax: _____

Address: _____

_____

Email: _____ Website: _____

Policy #: _____

Vehicle: _____

Year purchased:_____ Purchase price:_____

Insurance company: _____

Agent: _____

Phone: _____ Fax: _____

Address: _____

_____

Email: _____ Website: _____

Policy #: _____

Vehicle: _____

Year purchased:_____ Purchase price:_____

Insurance company: _____

Agent: _____

Phone: _____ Fax: _____

Address: _____

_____

Email: _____ Website: _____

Policy #: _____

Vehicle: _____

Year purchased:_____ Purchase price:_____

Insurance company: _____

Agent: _____

Phone: _____ Fax: _____

Address: _____

_____

Email: _____ Website: _____

Policy #: _____

Insurance: Other

The following miscellaneous information about my insurance may be of interest:

_____

_____

_____

_____

_____

_____

_____

_____

_____

_____

_____

_____

_____

_____

_____

_____

_____

_____

_____

_____

_____

_____

_____

_____

_____

_____

_____

_____

CHAPTER 4
RETIREMENT AND VETERANS BENEFITS

There are only two ways to live your life. One is as though nothing is a miracle. The other is as though everything is a miracle.

—Albert Einstein

Many of us receive, or will receive, income from Social Security, pensions, 401(k)s, and IRAs as well as benefits as a military veteran. Your family's eligibility for many of these benefits may depend on whether you are eligible. For example, if you are a veteran or have a pension or any retirement savings plans, your family may be entitled to significant benefits and financial security from those sources after your death. In this chapter, you can pull all that information together and find explanations of the various government and retirement benefits so you and your loved ones understand the options and how to access any benefits.

My To-Do Checklist

Done	Need to Do	
☐	☐	Assess Social Security benefits for you and your survivors
☐	☐	Check out benefits for veterans and their survivors
☐	☐	Record any workers' compensation benefits
☐	☐	Identify all available pension benefits

☐ ☐ Identify your retirement plans

☐ ☐ Verify and update the beneficiary designation on pension and retirement plans

☐ ☐ Complete the checklists for Chapter 4

✔ Assess Social Security benefits for you and your survivors

Social Security can be an important source of continuing income when your family's earnings are reduced or stopped because of your retirement, disability, or death.

Before you or your family can receive monthly cash benefits, you must be credited for a certain amount of work under Social Security. For most benefits, you must have at least ten years of Social Security-covered employment. Just how many credits you must establish depends on your age and whether you or your family is applying for retirement, survivor, or disability benefits. You can find details on specific requirements at www.ssa.gov or at any Social Security Administration (SSA) office located throughout the country. You can find those addresses at the SSA website or in the blue pages of your phone book.

You can start receiving retirement checks as early as age 62 and disability checks at any age. Be aware, however, that you will get up to a 30 percent reduction if you start receiving retirement benefits before your full retirement age. If you were born between 1943 and 1954, your full retirement age is 66. If you wait until age 70 to take Social Security retirement benefits, you get an additional amount. Check out the chart at www.ssa.gov/pubs/age increase.htm for more details on how your benefit amount changes based on when you start taking benefits. Keep in mind that your spouse will receive a significant reduction in the amount he or she will receive in survivor benefits if you start taking your retirement benefit early.

If you are receiving or are eligible to receive retirement benefits or are receiving disability benefits, your family members are also eligible for benefits under the following circumstances:

- Unmarried children under 18 (or 19 if a full-time elementary or secondary school student);
- Unmarried children 18 or over who were severely disabled before age 22, and who continue to be disabled;
- A wife or husband 62 or older who has been married to the worker for at least one year; or
- A wife or husband under 62 if she or he is caring for a child under 16 (or disabled) who is receiving a benefit under the worker's earnings.

A divorced spouse who has been divorced at least two years can receive benefits at age 62, regardless of whether the former spouse receives them. The marriage must have lasted ten years or more; the former spouse must be at least 62 and eligible for Social Security benefits, regardless of whether he or she has retired; and the divorced spouse must not be eligible for an equal or higher benefit on his or her own—or anyone else's—Social Security record.

A number of survivor benefits may be available to your surviving family members.

- Your spouse and minor children may be entitled to a one-time $255 lump sum payment.

Social Security survivors insurance can provide cash benefits based on your earnings record to the following:

- Your spouse can get full benefits at full retirement age, or reduced benefits as early as age 60;
- Your disabled spouse is eligible for benefits as early as age 50;
- Your spouse at any age if he or she takes care of your child who is under age 16 or disabled, and receiving Social Security benefits;
- Your unmarried children under 18, or up to age 19 if they are attending high school full time. Under certain circumstances, benefits can be paid to stepchildren, grandchildren, or adopted children;
- Your children at any age who were disabled before age 22 and remain disabled;
- Your dependent parents who are age 62 or older.

When your heirs go to the Social Security office to apply for their benefits, they will need to have your Social Security number along with copies of any marriage licenses, birth certificates, and other documents.

You can determine how much your family could receive in benefits after you die by checking your Social Security Statement. You can review your statement at any time by creating a MySocialSecurity account at https://secure.ssa.gov/RIL/SiView.do.

AARP's *Social Security for Dummies* by Jonathan Peterson (AARP.org/SS4 Dummies) is a good source of information concerning benefits for you and for your survivors.

Note: Because the Social Security Act is amended from time to time, contact the nearest Social Security office for a full explanation of your rights and those of your family under the law.

✔ Check out benefits for veterans and their survivors

The Department of Veterans Affairs (VA) is charged with administering benefits available to persons who have served on active duty in the U.S. military service. The available benefits depend upon the veteran's length of service, the era during which the service was performed, whether the veteran is disabled, whether the disability was caused by active service, and many other criteria.

You and your family will need to have documentation of your military service to apply for any benefits available to you or to your family. You can get a copy of your service record (DD-214) at www.archives.gov/veterans/military-service-records/get-service-records.html.

Under certain circumstances, the following benefits (and many more) *may* be available to you if you are a veteran:

- Pensions for disability caused by service-connected injury or disease
- Pensions for certain nonservice-connected disabilities
- Automobile allowance for service-connected loss or permanent loss of the use of one or both hands or feet
- Hospitalization benefits
- Help paying for the assistance of another in your home
- Alcohol and drug dependence treatment
- Nursing home care
- Outpatient medical treatment
- Prosthetic appliances
- Vocational rehabilitation and counseling
- Loan guaranty benefits
- Insurance
- Federal civil service preference

Many other services and benefits are available to your family following your death if you are an eligible veteran:

Burial flag. A U.S. flag may be issued to drape over your casket if you are an eligible veteran. After the funeral service, the flag may be given to your next of kin or close friend or associate. Flags are issued at any VA office and most local post offices. A Presidential Memorial Certificate is also available at no cost to your family.

Burial in national cemeteries. Burial in a national cemetery is open to all members of the U.S. Armed Forces and veterans having met minimum active service duty requirements and having been discharged under conditions other than dishonorable. Your spouse, widow or widower, minor children, and, under certain conditions, unmarried adult children are also eligible for burial in a national cemetery. An eligible spouse may be buried in a national cemetery, even if he or she predeceases you. In most cases, one gravesite is provided for the burial of all eligible family members and a single headstone or marker is provided. When both you and your spouse are veterans, you can request two gravesites and two headstones or markers. Certain members of the Armed Forces reserve components may also be eligible for burial depending on the space available. There is no charge for the grave plot, for its opening and closing, a grave liner, or for perpetual care.

Headstones or markers. The VA will furnish a government headstone or marker to be placed at your grave at any cemetery around the world. Even if the grave was previously marked, your family can obtain a government headstone. This service is provided for eligible veterans whether they are buried in a national cemetery or elsewhere. A headstone or marker is automatically furnished if burial is in a national cemetery. Otherwise, your family must apply to the VA. The VA will ship the headstone or marker, without charge, to the person or firm designated on the application. The VA will also furnish, on request, a medallion to place on an existing headstone or marker that indicates that the person was a veteran. Your family must pay the cost of setting the headstone or marker or attaching the medallion.

Military honors. By law, every eligible veteran may receive a military funeral honors ceremony, to include folding and presenting the U.S. burial flag and the playing of Taps. A military funeral honors detail consists of two or more uniformed military persons, with at least one being a member of your branch of the Armed Forces.

The Department of Defense program "Honoring Those Who Served" calls for funeral directors to request military funeral honors on behalf of your family. Veterans' organizations may assist in providing military funeral honors. In support of this program, VA national cemetery staff can help coordinate military funeral honors either at a national or private cemetery. For more information, go to www.militaryfuneralhonors.osd.mil/.

Reimbursement of burial expenses. The VA is authorized to pay an allowance toward your funeral and burial expenses if you are an eligible veteran. If it was a service-related death, the VA will pay up to $2,000 toward burial expenses. If you are to be buried in a VA national cemetery, some or all of the cost of transporting your body to the cemetery may be reimbursed. For a nonservice-related death, the VA will pay up to $300 toward burial and funeral expenses and a $300 plot-interment allowance. If your death happens while you are in a VA hospital or under VA contracted nursing home care, some or all of the costs for transporting your remains may be reimbursed.

Dependency and Indemnity Compensation (DIC). DIC payments may be authorized for your spouse, unmarried children, and low-income parents if you die during active duty or if your death is service-connected. The amount of the basic benefit is determined by your military pay grade. Payments are also made for children under age 18 or up to age 23 who are attending school.

Nonservice-connected death pension. Your surviving spouse and unmarried children under age 18 or up to age 23 who are attending school may be eligible for a pension if their income does not exceed certain limits.

Education for spouses, widows, widowers, sons, and daughters. If you are completely disabled or die as a result of your military service, the VA will generally (but with some exceptions) pay to help educate your spouse, widow or widower, and each son and daughter beyond the secondary school level, including college, graduate school, technical and vocational schools, apprenticeships, and on-the-job training programs. Education loans are also available through the VA.

✔ Record any workers' compensation benefits

All states have adopted workers' compensation laws. Although their details vary greatly, the general purpose of workers' compensation programs is to provide income to workers who are unable to work as a result of an injury or occupational disease while they are employed. While you are unable to work, you can receive a monetary benefit based on your average wage and number of dependents. In addition, your employer or the employer's insurance company will pay your medical expenses related to the injury.

You and your family should be alert to possible workers' compensation benefits available to your dependents. Ordinarily, if you die as the result of a work-incurred accident or occupational disease, your spouse and minor children are entitled to payments for a specified number of years or until your spouse's remarriage, whichever is sooner. Your dependent children are entitled to benefits until they reach a certain age.

Ordinarily, the laws also provide that your spouse or your estate are entitled to a specific funeral or death benefit.

In the checklists provided in this chapter, be sure to detail any of your medical problems, including life-threatening injuries or occupational diseases that may be related to your employment.

✔ Identify all available pension benefits

Many public and private employees are provided pensions through their jobs. Some pensions are entirely financed by the employer; others are cofinanced by the employer and the employee. Pensions are a way to accumulate tax-advantaged savings that you can tap for a steady stream of income when you are no longer working. Pensions are considered to be *defined benefit plans* because you receive a specific amount of money when you retire that is defined in the terms of the pension. To calculate how much you will receive, your plan uses a formula that includes your salary history and how many years you were eligible to receive pension benefits, called being vested in the pension. At the time you begin to receive your pension, you may have an opportunity to elect if your surviving spouse will continue to receive a portion of your pension after you die.

While many employers are no longer offering pensions, it's important for you to list all employment where you might have become eligible (vested) for a pension. You should check with all past employers that offered pension plans during your employment to determine if you or your survivors could receive any payments. Verify if survivor's benefits are available and check your designation of beneficiary. Refer to Chapter 3 for more information about naming beneficiaries.

✔ Identify your retirement plans

Many public and private employers offer ***401(k) retirement plans*** that defer taxes on both the contributions you and your employer make and the plan's earnings until you withdraw funds from the plan, usually when you retire. You will have to pay a 10 percent penalty on any money you withdraw before age 59½ in addition to income taxes.

These 401(k) plans are called ***defined contribution*** plans. You make a specific dollar contribution with each paycheck to a personal plan account. The plan invests your contributions (and your employer's, if any) in mutual funds or other investments that you select from the plan's menu of investment choices. Your plan account is credited with any returns on the investment.

You will also want to review any ***individual retirement accounts (IRAs)*** you hold. The law, as of 2014, allows a person who is under age 50 and who has earned income to deposit up to $5,500 into an IRA account each year ($6,500 for people over age 50). Contributions to your ***traditional*** IRA may be wholly or partially tax deductible or nondeductible depending on whether you are also covered by a qualified pension plan or a 401(k), your tax filing status, and your income level. Traditional IRAs delay having to pay taxes on earnings from contributions until you start to withdraw funds, usually when you retire. Again, tax penalties apply to early withdrawals before age 59½, except in certain circumstances. ***Roth*** IRA contributions, on the other hand, are not deductible, but withdrawals are tax free.

List any other tax-deferred plans you may have. These plans help you defer taxes until you have reached an age where most likely your earnings have begun to decline because you will be in a lower income tax bracket. For example, if you are self-employed, you may establish a Keogh plan, which allows for larger, tax-deferred yearly contributions and greater benefits than does an IRA. A ***SIMPLE*** IRA is a simplified plan, similar to a 401(k) plan, but with lower contribution limits and less costly administration. Another tax-deferred retirement for self-employed people is a simplified employee pension plan, or ***SEP***, which is a type of IRA.

Keep in mind that all of your retirement nest egg may not pass on to your heirs. Because your savings in retirement plans allow your money to grow without paying any taxes, the tax laws require you to start making withdrawals, and paying taxes, when you reach age 70½—or pay a penalty. If you haven't retired by age 70½, you must start taking withdrawals as soon as you retire. These withdrawals are called Required Minimum Distributions (RMDs). The RMD rules apply to all employer-sponsored retirement plans, including profit-sharing plans, 401(k) plans, 403(b) plans, and 457(b) plans. The RMD rules also apply to traditional IRAs and IRA-based plans such as SEPs, SARSEPs, and SIMPLE IRAs. The Internal Revenue Service (IRS) provides life expectancy tables and work sheets you can use to calculate the amount of your RMD in IRS Publication 590 at www .irs.gov/pub/irs-pdf/p590.pdf. The tax penalties for failing to take the correct RMDs are a stiff 50 percent. The Roth IRA rules are different because you have paid taxes on the money you contributed.

You can start taking withdrawals without penalty at any time after age 59½ and you can withdraw more than the required minimum amount.

If you die before age 70½, the beneficiaries of your 401(k) or IRA are also subject to special tax rules. Generally, the entire amount in your account must be distributed to an individual beneficiary either within five years of your death or over the life of the beneficiary, starting no later than one year following your death. Your beneficiaries will need to use the specific IRS life expectancy tables to calculate withdrawals and taxes and seek expert and timely advice on how best to manage this inheritance.

✔ Verify and update the beneficiary designation on pension and retirement plans

Be sure to verify that you have designated beneficiaries for every retirement savings plan. Review your beneficiary designations to make sure the listing accurately reflects who you want to receive any remaining funds in your plans.

Regardless of what type of retirement plans you are participating in, it is critical that your family is aware of those plans. At your death, one or more of those plans may provide payments to your spouse and/or minor children, or may provide a substantial payment to a designated beneficiary or to your estate. On the other hand, a plan may provide nothing at all to your survivors. The checklists in this chapter provide your heirs with the information they need about any retirement assets in which you—and they—have an interest.

Details about survivor benefits and all the details that loved ones need to pay attention to when someone dies can be found in *ABA/AARP Checklist for Family Survivors*, www.aarp .org/ChecklistforFamily.

Retirement and Veterans Benefits Action Checklists

The checklists in Chapter 4 are set out in the following order:

- *Pensions*
- *Retirement Plans*
- *Social Security Benefits*
- *Veterans Benefits*
- *Workers' Compensation*
- *Benefits: Other*

Pensions

☐ I do not have any rights to a pension.

☐ I have the following pensions:

Pension source: _____

Pension ID #:_____

Plan administrator: _____

Phone: _____ Fax: _____

Address: _____

_____

Email: _____ Website: _____

☐ There are benefits to survivors under this plan.

☐ There are no benefits to survivors under this plan.

Pension source: _____

Pension ID #:_____

Plan administrator: _____

Phone: _____ Fax: _____

Address: _____

_____

Email: _____ Website: _____

☐ There are benefits to survivors under this plan.

☐ There are no benefits to survivors under this plan.

Pension source: _____

Pension ID #:_____

Plan administrator: _____

Phone: _____ Fax: _____

Address: _____

_____

Email: _____ Website: _____

☐ There are benefits to survivors under this plan.

☐ There are no benefits to survivors under this plan.

Pension source: _____

Pension ID #:_____

Plan administrator: _____

Phone: _____ Fax: _____

Address: _____

_____

Email: _____ Website: _____

    ☐ There are benefits to survivors under this plan.

    ☐ There are no benefits to survivors under this plan.

Pension source: _____

Pension ID #:_____

Plan administrator: _____

Phone: _____ Fax: _____

Address: _____

_____

Email: _____ Website: _____

    ☐ There are benefits to survivors under this plan.

    ☐ There are no benefits to survivors under this plan.

Pension source: _____

Pension ID #:_____

Plan administrator: _____

Phone: _____ Fax: _____

Address: _____

_____

Email: _____ Website: _____

    ☐ There are benefits to survivors under this plan.

    ☐ There are no benefits to survivors under this plan.

Retirement Plans

    ☐ I do not have an individual retirement account (IRA).

    ☐ I do have the following individual retirement accounts (IRAs):

Financial institution holding my IRA: _____

IRA account #: _____

Phone: _____ Fax: _____

Address: _____

_____

Email: _____ Website: _____

    ☐ There are benefits to survivors under this plan.

    ☐ There are no benefits to survivors under this plan.

Financial institution holding my IRA: _____

IRA account #: _____

Phone: _____ Fax: _____

Address: _____

_____

Email: _____ Website: _____

    ☐ There are benefits to survivors under this plan.

    ☐ There are no benefits to survivors under this plan.

****

☐ I do not have a 401(k) plan.

☐ I do have the following 401(k) plans:

Financial institution/Plan administrator:_____

Account #: _____

Phone: _____ Fax: _____

Address: _____

_____

Email: _____ Website: _____

☐ There are benefits to survivors under this plan.

☐ There are no benefits to survivors under this plan.

****

☐ I do not have a 403(b) plan.

☐ I do have the following 403(b) plans:

Financial institution/Plan administrator:_____

Account #: _____

Phone: _____ Fax: _____

Address: _____

_____

Email: _____ Website: _____

☐ There are benefits to survivors under this plan.

☐ There are no benefits to survivors under this plan.

****

☐ I do not have a Keogh plan.

☐ I do have the following Keogh plan:

Financial institution/Plan administrator: _____

Account #: _____

Phone: _____ Fax: _____

Address: _____

_____

Email: _____ Website: _____

☐ There are benefits to survivors under this plan.

☐ There are no benefits to survivors under this plan.

****

☐ I do not have a Simplified Employee Pension (SEP) plan.

☐ I do have the following SEP plan:

Financial institution/Plan administrator: _____

Account #: _____

Phone: _____ Fax: _____

Address: _____

_____

Email: _____ Website: _____

☐ There are benefits to survivors under this plan.

☐ There are no benefits to survivors under this plan.

****

☐   I do not have a Roth IRA.

☐   I do have the following Roth IRA:

Financial institution/Plan administrator:_____

Account #: _____

Phone: _____ Fax: _____

Address: _____

_____

Email: _____ Website: _____

☐   There are benefits to survivors under this plan.

☐   There are no benefits to survivors under this plan.

Social Security Benefits

☐ I am eligible for Social Security benefits.

☐ I am not eligible for Social Security benefits.

☐ I receive monthly Social Security benefits.

☐ I worked in the railroad industry at any time after January 1, 1937.*

☐ I did not work in the railroad industry at any time after January 1, 1937.

Name on Social Security card: _____

Social Security Number: _____

Type of monthly Social Security benefit: _____

(Disability, Retirement, Widow, etc.)

Monthly Social Security benefit amount: _____

Estimate of amount my surviving dependents would receive: _____

My Social Security benefit is deposited at: _____

(Bank)

This may affect the amount of Social Security you receive.

Veterans Benefits

☐ I did not serve in the U.S. military.

☐ I served in the U.S. military.

Name served under: _____

First   Middle   Last

Military service number (DD-214): _____

I entered active service on: _____

I was separated from active service on: _____

Branch: _____

Grade or rank: _____

National Guard: _____

Reserves: _____

The following is a resume of my military career:

_____

_____

_____

_____

_____

_____

_____

_____

_____

_____

_____

_____

_____

_____

_____

_____

_____

_____

Workers' Compensation

☐   I have never received workers' compensation benefits.

☐   I receive or have received the following workers' compensation benefits.

☐   My survivors may be eligible for workers' compensation benefits:

Employer: _____

Phone: _____ Fax: _____

Address: _____

_____

Email: _____ Website: _____

****

Date of injury or occupational disease:_____

Insurance company: _____

Phone: _____ Fax: _____

Address: _____

_____

Email: _____ Website: _____

Claim #:_____

Details of injury or occupational disease:

_____

_____

_____

****

In addition to the above, I received the following injuries or occupational diseases during my employment:

_____

_____

_____

Benefits: Other

The following miscellaneous information about public benefits may be of interest:

_____

_____

_____

_____

_____

_____

_____

_____

_____

_____

_____

_____

_____

_____

_____

_____

_____

_____

_____

_____

_____

_____

_____

_____

_____

_____

_____

_____

_____

_____

_____

_____

CHAPTER 5
BANKING AND SAVINGS

*You have achieved success if you have lived well,
laughed often, and loved much.*

—Author Unknown

Banks used to be pretty plain vanilla. They offered checking and savings accounts, lent money to buy homes and cars, and maybe gave you a toaster when you opened a new account. Now you probably take advantage of a proliferation of services and have multiple types of accounts. In addition to a checking account and a savings account, you might have a certificate of deposit or money market account; carry a credit card or debit card with a PIN (personal identification number); use a financial adviser housed in the bank; rely on the automatic teller machine (ATM) to withdraw cash and transfer funds between accounts; and pay your bills online. Thanks to interstate banking, you may use different banks for different types of services. However and wherever you bank, your family needs to know about all the different types of accounts, where they are located, account numbers, PINs, etc. This chapter will help you set out all that information.

As part of your estate planning, it's essential that you understand the different ways you can own your bank accounts. To help you plan, I've also included a primer on the various types of banking products and the ways accounts can be titled, which determines who gets the money in the account.

My To-Do Checklist

Done	Need to Do	
☐	☐	Review how bank accounts are titled
☐	☐	List all banks where you do business

☐	☐	List any credit unions where you do business
☐	☐	Assemble account numbers and—with caution—your access PINs, ATM passwords, online banking usernames, and passwords
☐	☐	Keep a record of all savings bonds
☐	☐	Make sure that your accounts are FDIC insured
☐	☐	Keep original documents that are valuable or irreplaceable in a safe deposit box
☐	☐	Be sure that someone knows where safe deposit boxes and keys are located
☐	☐	Complete the checklists for Chapter 5

✔ Review how bank accounts are titled

How you title, or own, your various bank accounts can make a big difference for your heirs and who will be entitled to the money on deposit when you die. Among the possible ways you can own bank accounts are these:

Individually: Money retaining in this account will be distributed according to the terms of your will, or if you do not have a will, according to state law.

Agency or convenience account: A co-signer can access money in this type of account but the money in the account does not belong to the co-signer on your death. This is the type of account most people should use if they want a family member to have access to the account to help pay bills when they are out of town or in the hospital. Money remaining in this account will be distributed according to the terms of your will, or if you do not have a will, according to state law.

Joint with right of survivorship: As soon as you create a joint account with right of survivorship, all money in the account belongs to you and the co-owner and on your death automatically goes to the surviving co-owner. Adding a son, daughter, or any other person to your account as joint owner is the same as making a gift of all money now on deposit and any future deposits. The co-owner can write checks for any purpose and could, in fact, withdraw it to zero and head for Alaska. For Medicaid purposes, adding a joint owner (other than your spouse) to an account is considered a transfer for less than fair market value and could result in delaying your eligibility for Medicaid.

Pay on death (POD): The person you name as beneficiary on this type of account automatically receives the balance in the account on your death but has no right or authority to access the account until then. You can change the beneficiary, spend the money, or close the account at any time. Some people use a POD account to set aside money to pay funeral expenses.

✔ List all banks where you do business

Commercial banks offer a wide range of services. They handle savings and checking accounts and make short- and long-term loans for personal and business use. Many also provide estate and investment services.

Checking accounts are considered **demand deposits**. In other words, as the depositor, you have the right to demand, or to withdraw, any or all of your funds at any time during regular banking hours. Many financial institutions now offer interest-bearing checking accounts, along with traditional fee-based checking plans. Most banks charge stiff fees for each overdrawn check. They may offer overdraft protection by linking your checking account to your savings account, although some institutions will charge a fee for overdraft protection. Be sure you understand what fees your bank will collect for overdraft protection or overdrawn checks.

Savings accounts are another type of demand deposit. Savings accounts pay you interest, which is noted, along with deposits and withdrawals, on a periodic statement or available on online.

Money market savings accounts pay a higher rate of interest than a standard savings account but may require you to maintain a certain minimum balance in your account.

Certificates of deposit are **time deposits**. Customers who use certificates of deposit (CDs) agree to leave their money in the bank for a certain period—for example, two years. During that time, you may not withdraw those funds without incurring significant interest penalties. In return for having this long-term use of your money, banks generally pay a higher rate of interest than they would for savings accounts.

Factors that affect the interest you can earn on your deposit accounts include your bank's method of compounding interest and of crediting the funds you put in the account and the money you withdraw. Banks can compound interest in a variety of ways, so it pays to compare the details before opening a savings account or buying a CD.

✔ List any credit unions where you do business

Credit unions work very much like banks, although they are organized differently from banking institutions. Typically you need to be a member of some identified group to have an account, but in turn you become a part owner of the credit union, along with all the other depositors. Credit unions offer services that encourage you to save and often provide its members loans at lower rates. They offer checking and savings accounts (although they may be called share or draft accounts), credit cards, and online banking. Federally chartered credit unions are regulated by the National Credit Union Administration. Check to make sure your credit union account is insured by the National Credit Union Share Insurance Fund (NCUSIF). Like the FDIC, the NCUSIF insures credit union accounts up to $250,000. You can find or check out a credit union at www.ncua.gov/DataApps/ResearchCU/Pages /default.aspx.

✔ **Assemble account numbers and—with caution—your access PINs, ATM passwords, online banking usernames, and passwords**

With today's multiple ways to do banking, we can accumulate a sometimes bewildering collection of cards, personal identification numbers, passwords, and usernames. These are the keys that you use to do your banking without ever entering a bank. You use them to get cash from an ATM or transfer funds and pay bills via online banking.

But beware: They are also the very valuable keys that others can use to raid your accounts. You need to be extraordinarily careful about lending your ATM card, keeping your PIN private, and creating your passwords. For example, don't record your PIN on a piece of paper that you carry next to your debit card. Make sure that no one is looking over your shoulder when you enter your pass code at an ATM. Change your passwords frequently and avoid something that would be obvious to a hacker, such as your mother's maiden name, birth date, or child's name. Identity thieves can easily find this information about you on the Internet, on social networking, school alumni, or genealogical sites. Using numbers, symbols, and a mix of uppercase and lowercase letters can help you build stronger passwords. For tips on creating safe passwords and more, see AARP's *Protecting Yourself Online for Dummies* e-book at AARP.org/ProtectingYourselfOnline.

✔ **Keep a record of all savings bonds**

Savings bonds are a very easy and secure way to save. You should make a list of each bond you are holding, the type series (E, EE, H, HH, or I), denomination, and issue date. Your heirs will find this list very helpful.

Depending on what type of savings bonds you have purchased and their maturity date, they may still be earning interest, or just sitting at maturity and no longer growing. There is more than $15 billion in unredeemed bonds. The U.S. Treasury Department does not send out notices when bonds have reached maturity and stopped earning interest, but it is easy to find out. You can use the Treasury Hunt tool on the web at www.savingsbonds.gov/indiv /tools/tools_treasuryhunt.htm to find out how much each bond is worth today. The Treasury Hunt tool lists bonds that have reached final maturity and were issued after 1974. This site will also tell you how to file claims for lost, stolen, destroyed, or undelivered bonds.

You may want to consider moving your mature savings bonds to a TreasuryDirect account where the proceeds will be deposited to a Certificate of Indebtedness. Find out more about how this works at Smart Exchange, www.treasurydirect.gov/indiv/research /indepth/smartexchangeinfo.htm.

✔ Make sure that your accounts are FDIC insured

Most banks insure their deposits through the Federal Deposit Insurance Corporation (FDIC). This governmental agency was established to protect people from losing their deposited assets if a bank fails. Up to $250,000 in your account is insured. Be sure that your bank is insured by the FDIC and check the coverage limits on your accounts. Use the FDIC's EDIE (Electronic Deposit Insurance Estimator) calculator at www.fdic.gov/edie/ index.html.

The FDIC insurance covers deposit accounts, including checking and savings accounts, money market deposit accounts, certificates of deposit, and IRA accounts. It does not insure any other type of investment products you might purchase through your bank, such as mutual funds. If the total amount of your deposits exceeds the maximum amount of deposit insurance, you can establish accounts in several name combinations (for example, husband alone, husband and wife, wife alone, husband and child) or, if necessary, in several banks.

✔ Keep original documents that are valuable or irreplaceable in a safe deposit box

✔ Be sure that someone knows where safe deposit boxes and keys are located

Safe deposit boxes provide a place for storing valuables and documents at a small cost. Safe deposit boxes protect your stocks, bonds, gold, silver, and other valuables from both physical burglary and fire damage. You may want to store in your safe deposit box important papers such as your marriage license, deeds to your real estate, car titles, and insurance policies. Be sure to record what is in your safe deposit box in the Where to Find It Checklist starting on page 35.

Most banks rent safe deposit boxes for a yearly fee or provide them as a free service or at a discounted cost depending on the type of checking or savings accounts you have. Safe deposit boxes come with a key. When you want to store items or access items, you must use both your key and a bank key simultaneously. Neither key alone will open the box for safety precautions. For further protection, you must also provide your signature and identification each time you seek access to the box. Your signature will be compared to the signature that you placed on file when you first rented the box.

To protect you and the property in your box, banks restrict who can get into your box, as well as when and how they can do so. These security protections may hinder your family's need to have ready and easy access to your will or advance directives, so you won't want to keep your will and advance directives in your safe deposit box.

A safe deposit box, like a bank account, may be owned in your name only or jointly. Joint ownership gives someone else access to your box should you need to get something out of the box when you are sick or out of town. In addition, joint ownership allows the co-owner access to the box after your death.

Most states require the bank to seal a safe deposit box upon learning of the death of an owner or co-owner. They then allow a surviving co-owner or the executor to open the box in the presence of a bank or government official. An inventory of all the contents needs to be made and delivered to the probate court. This process ensures that your assets are properly reported to the court and that the applicable estate or inheritance taxes are applied to the contents of the box.

While joint owners of a safe deposit box have access to the box, access does not mean that they own the contents of the box. Putting your diamond ring into a safe deposit box does not change the ring's owner or make a gift of the ring to the joint owner of the box. The ring will be part of your probate estate. If you have any questions about the rights of a co-owner to your box, check with your bank or your lawyer.

Banking and Savings
Action Checklists

The checklists in Chapter 5 are set out in the following order:

- *Certificates of Deposit*
- *Checking Accounts*
- *Credit Unions*
- *Safe Deposit Boxes*
- *Savings Accounts*
- *Savings Bonds*
- *Banking and Savings: Other*

Certificates of Deposit

☐ I do not have any certificates of deposit (CDs).

☐ I have the following certificates of deposit (CDs):

Name of institution: _____

Account #:_____

Maturity date: _____

Phone: _____ Fax: _____

Address: _____

_____

Email: _____ Website: _____

Name of institution: _____

Account #:_____

Maturity date: _____

Phone: _____ Fax: _____

Address: _____

_____

Email: _____ Website: _____

Name of institution: _____

Account #:_____

Maturity date: _____

Phone: _____ Fax: _____

Address: _____

_____

Email: _____ Website: _____

Name of institution: _____

Account #: _____

Maturity date: _____

Phone: _____ Fax: _____

Address: _____

_____

Email: _____ Website: _____

Name of institution: _____

Account #: _____

Maturity date: _____

Phone: _____ Fax: _____

Address: _____

_____

Email: _____ Website: _____

Name of institution: _____

Account #: _____

Maturity date: _____

Phone: _____ Fax: _____

Address: _____

_____

Email: _____ Website: _____

Name of institution: _____

Account #: _____

Maturity date: _____

Phone: _____ Fax: _____

Address: _____

_____

Email: _____ Website: _____

Checking Accounts

    ☐ I do not have any checking accounts.

    ☐ I have the following checking accounts:

Name of institution: _____

Phone: _____ Fax: _____

Address: _____

_____

Website: _____

Account #: _____

ATM PIN #: _____

Online banking user ID: _____

Online banking password: _____

Name of institution: _____

Phone: _____ Fax: _____

Address: _____

_____

Website: _____

Account #: _____

ATM PIN #: _____

Online banking user ID: _____

Online banking password: _____

Name of institution: _____

Phone: _____ Fax: _____

Address: _____

_____

Website: _____

Account #: _____

ATM PIN #: _____

Online banking user ID: _____

Online banking password: _____

© American Bar Association

Name of institution: _____

Phone: _____ Fax: _____

Address: _____

_____

Website:_____

Account #:_____

ATM PIN #:_____

Online banking user ID: _____

Online banking password:_____

Name of institution: _____

Phone: _____ Fax: _____

Address: _____

_____

Website:_____

Account #:_____

ATM PIN #:_____

Online banking user ID: _____

Online banking password:_____

Name of institution: _____

Phone: _____ Fax: _____

Address: _____

_____

Website:_____

Account #:_____

ATM PIN #:_____

Online banking user ID: _____

Online banking password:_____

Credit Unions

☐   I do not have any credit union accounts.

☐   I have the following credit union accounts:

Name of institution: _____

Phone: _____ Fax: _____

Address: _____

_____

Website: _____

Account #: _____

ATM PIN #: _____

Online user ID: _____

Online password: _____

Name of institution: _____

Phone: _____ Fax: _____

Address: _____

_____

Website: _____

Account #: _____

ATM PIN #: _____

Online user ID: _____

Online password: _____

Name of institution: _____

Phone: _____ Fax: _____

Address: _____

_____

Website: _____

Account #: _____

ATM PIN #: _____

Online user ID: _____

Online password: _____

Safe Deposit Boxes

☐ I do not have any safe deposit boxes.

☐ I have the following safe deposit boxes:

Name of institution: _____

Phone: _____ Fax: _____

Address: _____

_____

Email: _____ Website: _____

Box #: _____

Key location: _____

Box rent: _____

Things I have stored in this box:

_____

_____

_____

_____

Name of institution: _____

Phone: _____ Fax: _____

Address: _____

_____

Email: _____ Website: _____

Box #: _____

Key location: _____

Box rent: _____

Things I have stored in this box:

_____

_____

_____

_____

Name of institution: _____

Phone: _____ Fax: _____

Address: _____

_____

Email: _____ Website: _____

Box #: _____

Key location: _____

Box rent: _____

Things I have stored in this box:

_____

_____

_____

_____

Name of institution: _____

Phone: _____ Fax: _____

Address: _____

_____

Email: _____ Website: _____

Box #: _____

Key location: _____

Box rent: _____

Things I have stored in this box:

_____

_____

_____

_____

Also record what you have in your safe deposit box on the Where to Find It Checklist beginning on page 35.

Savings Accounts

☐   I do not have any savings accounts.

☐   I have the following savings accounts:

Name of institution: _____

Account #:_____

Phone: _____ Fax: _____

Address: _____

_____

Website:_____

Name of institution: _____

Account #:_____

Phonc: _____ Fax: _____

Address: _____

_____

Website:_____

Name of institution: _____

Account #:_____

Phone: _____ Fax: _____

Address: _____

_____

Website:_____

Name of institution: _____

Account #:_____

Phone: _____ Fax: _____

Address: _____

_____

Website:_____

Savings Bonds

    ☐ I do not have any savings bonds.

    ☐ I have an Individual TreasuryDirect account:

Account name: _____

Password: _____

Account #: _____

    ☐ I have the following savings bonds:

    ☐ My savings bonds are located: _____

Series	Denomination	Serial Number	Issue Date

Banking and Savings: Other

The following miscellaneous information about my banking and savings may be of interest:

_____

_____

_____

_____

_____

_____

_____

_____

_____

_____

_____

_____

_____

_____

_____

_____

_____

_____

_____

_____

_____

_____

_____

_____

_____

_____

_____

_____

_____

_____

CHAPTER 6
INVESTMENTS

Life is either a daring adventure or nothing.

—Helen Keller

You have multiple ways you can invest for your own financial security and build up resources to leave for your family. Whether you actively follow the stock market, use online trading, rely on a financial adviser, or keep your nest egg in mutual funds and certificates of deposit, you most likely have two basic goals. One is to have enough money throughout your retirement to cover your expenses comfortably. The other is to be able to have enough left over to take care of your loved ones.

You can use the checklists in this chapter as a convenient place to record information about the securities you own, where you have investment accounts, and how your family can contact your brokers or financial advisers. This chapter briefly covers some of the ways you can invest your money, including stocks, bonds, and mutual funds.

My To-Do Checklist

Done	Need to Do	
☐	☐	Periodically check to make sure your investments match your investment objectives and are diversified
☐	☐	Check on the background of any financial professional
☐	☐	Organize statements you receive from your brokerage firm or investment adviser
☐	☐	Complete the checklists for Chapter 6

✔ **Periodically check to make sure your investments match your investment objectives and are diversified**

Stocks

When you own a stock, you own part of a company. Companies sell these pieces of ownership, known as shares, to raise money to finance their business. When you buy a stock, you are basically betting that the company will grow. As the company does well, your stock generally increases in value. You can earn money on your investment when either the price of the stock rises or if the company shares profits by paying a dividend. If the company does poorly, you can lose some or all of the money you paid for the share.

There are more than 3,000 companies that you can invest in listed on the New York Stock Exchange. Stocks are categorized in multiple ways: by industry (auto, biotechnology); by market sector (utilities, health care); or geography (U.S., Asian). They can also be categorized by size, as in large-capitalization, or large-cap (generally companies worth more than $5 billion), mid-cap ($1 to $5 billion), or small-cap ($250 million to $1 billion). Another way to group stocks is based on financial experts' perception of the company's basic financial health and historical performance. These categories include growth stocks, value stocks, or income stocks. Knowing how a particular company's stocks are categorized helps you diversify your investments in different types of companies. Diversification reduces your risk of losing money.

Bonds

When you buy a bond, you loan money to a business or government entity. The entity commits to paying you interest at a fixed rate for the life of the loan and to return to you the value of the loan by a certain date, called the maturity date. When you invest in a bond, you are taking the risk that the entity may not be able to pay the interest or the principal. You also run the risk that if interest rates rise and you need to sell the bond, your bond may lose value. This is because other investors can buy higher rate bonds, so you have to sell yours at a lower price to attract a buyer. If you buy a *callable* bond, the company has the right to pay you back before the maturity date. This is normally done when the company can borrow at a cheaper rate.

Bonds issued by the federal government are the safest. Treasury bills, notes, and bonds are available with maturities ranging from one to thirty years. They can be easily sold, but like all bonds their values rise and fall as interest rates change. You pay no federal income tax on the interest you earn.

State and local governments also issue bonds to pay for things like roads, schools, and public safety. You pay no federal income tax on the interest, and you may not have to pay state taxes if you live in the area where the bond is issued. Because of this tax advantage, the interest rates on governmental or municipal bonds are lower than on other types of bonds.

Mutual Funds

When you buy shares of a mutual fund, you own a bit of various stocks, bonds, or other types of investments in the fund. Buying shares of a mutual fund helps you diversify because you are spreading the risk of losing your money among many different investments. Investments within a mutual fund are chosen by a professional manager based on the fund's investment objectives. The fund's objectives, set out in a public document called a prospectus, might be to own growth stock or government bonds or invest in a particular industry, such as pharmaceuticals.

Morningstar, a provider of mutual fund research, tracks more than 15,000 mutual funds. These are some of the common types of mutual funds:

- Stock funds invest in the stocks of many companies;
- Bond funds are a collection of bonds purchased with pooled money from many investors;
- Money market funds include short-term, low-risk loans;
- Balanced funds include a mix of stocks and bonds;
- Life cycle funds, or target retirement date funds, are designed to increase the percentage of bonds in relation to stocks as the investor gets closer to retirement age.

Money market accounts and money market funds have significant differences. A *money market account* is a type of saving account you have at a financial institution. Typically the financial institution will pay a higher rate of interest than on regular savings accounts. You are able to make withdrawals at any time and can access the funds through ATM withdrawals or by writing a check. As with other accounts in FDIC-insured banks, your money would be insured up to $250,000. You may have to maintain a minimum amount to avoid fees and be restricted on how many withdrawals you can make in a month. A *money market fund* is a type of mutual fund that is required by law to invest in low-risk, short-term debt. These funds are not insured.

Index funds or Exchange Traded Funds (ETF) are similar investment funds to mutual funds. They try to replicate the performance of an index, such as the Standard & Poor's 500 index, by investing in all the securities in that index. This is called passive management, which results in lower management fees than mutual funds.

As with any type of investment, you need to carefully match the fund's objectives with your own investment objectives. You also need to pay attention to the fund's fees. High fees or expense ratios can reduce your earnings.

Checklist for My Family: A Guide to My History, Financial Plans, and Final Wishes

College Savings Plans (529 Plans)

A 529 plan is an education savings plan operated by a state or educational institution designed to help families set aside funds for future college costs. You could set up a 529 account to create or contribute to a college savings plan for your children or grandchildren. It is named after Section 529 of the Internal Revenue Code, which created these types of savings plans. College savings plans can be used to meet the costs of qualified colleges nationwide. In most plans, the student can attend schools either in or out of the state where the 529 plan is located. It's up to each state to set up its own program, but most states have at least one type of plan.

You can get federal and most likely state tax benefits by contributing to the plan. You can take money out of the plan that you've contributed should an emergency arise and you need the money, but there will be tax consequences. Money you've contributed to a 529 plan is considered a completed gift, so the money in the plan is not part of your probate estate. Some states, however, may consider the money you have contributed to a 529 plan as an available asset, or "countable resource," in determining whether you are eligible for Medicaid. Check with an elder law attorney about the Medicaid rules in your state.

It's recommended that when you set up a 529 plan, you name a successor owner, so when you die the account continues automatically under the new owner. If you don't name a successor, the probate court will need to name the new owner, although some states have rules about who would become the new owner. Under most circumstances, the new owner would have the same rights that you had to change beneficiaries and disburse or withdraw funds.

✔ Check on the background of any financial professional

Many different types of professionals can assist you in managing your investments, developing an investment strategy, or in setting up an estate plan and a withdrawal plan from your pension or other retirement account. Which type of professional you should consult depends on what investment help you need.

Certified Public Accountants (CPAs) are licensed by a state to offer a variety of accounting services including tax preparation, financial audits, business valuations, and succession planning for small businesses.

Enrolled agents are federally licensed tax preparers who are qualified to represent you before the Internal Revenue Service. They have passed a comprehensive IRS examination or are former IRS employees.

Estate planning lawyers can draft legal documents for you including your will and power of attorney or develop wealth transfer strategies to ensure your estate passes to your heirs in the most tax-efficient manner.

138

Fee-only advisers are paid a specific fee for each service.

Financial planners generally take a broad view of your financial affairs. They may develop a comprehensive plan to meet your investment goals or generally advise you on financial matters. They may also manage your investment portfolio.

Insurance agents can help you with your insurance needs including health, long-term care, and life insurance as well as annuities.

Investment advisers generally focus on managing your investments. Most are paid by taking a percentage of the assets they manage for you.

Stockbrokers buy and sell stocks and bonds and are paid by commissions on the trades they make for you. Some brokers also provide financial planning services.

Before hiring any financial professional, always ask what licenses or certifications they hold, the types of services they offer, the typical clients they work with, and how they will be compensated. You should always know in advance how and how much you are going to pay for your financial professional's services. Get in writing whether you are paying a retainer fee upfront, being charged a set fee for each service, or having a percentage deducted from any transaction.

You can often get information on professionals using online resources:

- Attorneys: your state bar association's website
- Brokerages, brokers, and investment advisers: www.finra.org/brokercheck
- Certified Financial Planners: www.cfp.net/search
- Disciplinary actions taken against CPAs: www.aicpa.org/FORTHEPUBLIC /DISCIPLINARYACTIONS/Pages/default.aspx
- Insurance agents: www.naic.org
- Investment advisers: www.adviserinfo.sec.gov

✔ Organize statements you receive from your brokerage firm or investment adviser

While much investing can be done online, keeping track of your investments still involves lots of paper. You can accumulate a small mountain of paper associated with prospectuses, proxy notices, annual reports, and monthly and quarterly statements.

I keep a big 3-inch binder for my brokerage statements. To save on space, I throw away the monthly statements when I get my quarterly statement, and then throw away the quarterly statements when the annual summary comes in. Another way to save on paper is to request electronic statements and notices and save them to a folder. By organizing your investment information, you will lessen the work that your family members will have to do when they need to manage your investments.

Investments
Action Checklists

The checklists in Chapter 6 are set out in the following order:

- *Bonds*
- *College Savings Plans (529 Plans)*
- *Money Market Funds*
- *Municipal Bonds*
- *Mutual Funds*
- *Stocks*
- *Treasury Bills and Bonds*
- *Investments: Other*

Bonds

☐   I do not have any bonds or bond funds.

☐   I have the following bonds or bond funds:

Name of institution/Brokerage firm: _____

Account #: _____

Phone: _____ Fax: _____

Address: _____

_____

Email: _____ Website: _____

Name of institution/Brokerage firm: _____

Account #: _____

Phone: _____ Fax: _____

Address: _____

_____

Email: _____ Website: _____

Name of institution/Brokerage firm: _____

Account #: _____

Phone: _____ Fax: _____

Address: _____

_____

Email: _____ Website: _____

Name of institution/Brokerage firm: _____

Account #: _____

Phone: _____ Fax: _____

Address: _____

_____

Email: _____ Website: _____

College Savings Plans (529 Plans)

☐   I have not contributed to any college savings plans.

☐   I have contributed to the following college savings plans:

Name of institution/Brokerage firm:_____

Beneficiary:_____

Successor owner: _____

Account #:_____

Phone: _____ Fax: _____

Address: _____

_____

Email: _____ Website: _____

Name of institution/Brokerage firm:_____

Beneficiary:_____

Successor owner: _____

Account #:_____

Phone: _____ Fax: _____

Address: _____

_____

Email: _____ Website: _____

Name of institution/Brokerage firm:_____

Beneficiary:_____

Successor owner: _____

Account #:_____

Phone: _____ Fax: _____

Address: _____

_____

Email: _____ Website: _____

Money Market Funds

☐ I do not have any money market funds.

☐ I have the following money market funds:

Name of institution/Brokerage firm: _____

Account #: _____

Phone: _____ Fax: _____

Address: _____

_____

Email: _____ Website: _____

Name of institution/Brokerage firm: _____

Account #: _____

Phone: _____ Fax: _____

Address: _____

_____

Email: _____ Website: _____

Name of institution/Brokerage firm: _____

Account #: _____

Phone: _____ Fax: _____

Address: _____

_____

Email: _____ Website: _____

Name of institution/Brokerage firm: _____

Account #: _____

Phone: _____ Fax: _____

Address: _____

_____

Email: _____ Website: _____

Municipal Bonds

☐   I do not have any municipal bonds.

☐   I have the following municipal bonds:

Name of institution/Brokerage firm:_____

Account #:_____

Phone: _____ Fax: _____

Address: _____

_____

Email: _____ Website: _____

Name of institution/Brokerage firm:_____

Account #:_____

Phone: _____ Fax: _____

Address: _____

_____

Email: _____ Website: _____

Name of institution/Brokerage firm:_____

Account #:_____

Phone: _____ Fax: _____

Address: _____

_____

Email: _____ Website: _____

Name of institution/Brokerage firm:_____

Account #:_____

Phone: _____ Fax: _____

Address: _____

_____

Email: _____ Website: _____

Mutual Funds

☐ I do not have any mutual funds.

☐ I have the following mutual funds:

Name of institution/Brokerage firm: _____

Account #: _____

Phone: _____ Fax: _____

Address: _____

_____

Email: _____ Website: _____

Name of institution/Brokerage firm: _____

Account #: _____

Phone: _____ Fax: _____

Address: _____

_____

Email: _____ Website: _____

Name of institution/Brokerage firm: _____

Account #: _____

Phone: _____ Fax: _____

Address: _____

_____

Email: _____ Website: _____

Name of institution/Brokerage firm: _____

Account #: _____

Phone: _____ Fax: _____

Address: _____

_____

Email: _____ Website: _____

Stocks

 ☐ I do not have any stocks.

 ☐ I have the following stocks:

Name of institution/Brokerage firm:_____

Account #:_____

Phone: _____ Fax: _____

Address: _____

_____

Email: _____ Website: _____

Name of institution/Brokerage firm:_____

Account #:_____

Phone: _____ Fax: _____

Address: _____

_____

Email: _____ Website: _____

Name of institution/Brokerage firm:_____

Account #:_____

Phone: _____ Fax: _____

Address: _____

_____

Email: _____ Website: _____

Name of institution/Brokerage firm:_____

Account #:_____

Phone: _____ Fax: _____

Address: _____

_____

Email: _____ Website: _____

Name of institution/Brokerage firm: _____

Account #: _____

Phone: _____ Fax: _____

Address: _____

_____

Email: _____ Website: _____

Name of institution/Brokerage firm: _____

Account #: _____

Phone: _____ Fax: _____

Address: _____

_____

Email: _____ Website: _____

Name of institution/Brokerage firm: _____

Account #: _____

Phone: _____ Fax: _____

Address: _____

_____

Email: _____ Website: _____

Name of institution/Brokerage firm: _____

Account #: _____

Phone: _____ Fax: _____

Address: _____

_____

Email: _____ Website: _____

Treasury Bills and Bonds

☐   I do not have any Treasury bills or bonds.

☐   I have the following Treasury bills or bonds funds:

Name of institution/Brokerage firm: _____

Account #: _____

Phone: _____ Fax: _____

Address: _____

_____

Email: _____ Website: _____

Name of institution/Brokerage firm: _____

Account #: _____

Phone: _____ Fax: _____

Address: _____

_____

Email: _____ Website: _____

Name of institution/Brokerage firm: _____

Account #: _____

Phone: _____ Fax: _____

Address: _____

_____

Email: _____ Website: _____

Name of institution/Brokerage firm: _____

Account #: _____

Phone: _____ Fax: _____

Address: _____

_____

Email: _____ Website: _____

Investments: Other

The following miscellaneous information about my investments may be of interest:

_____

_____

_____

_____

_____

_____

_____

_____

_____

_____

_____

_____

_____

_____

_____

_____

_____

_____

_____

_____

_____

_____

_____

_____

_____

_____

_____

_____

_____

_____

CHAPTER 7
REAL ESTATE

*He is a wise man who does not grieve for the things
which he has not, but rejoices for those which he has.*

—Marcel Proust

Real estate, or **real property,** is everything permanently attached to the land that you own. When you buy real estate, you not only purchase land, but also the buildings, trees, fences, and water that are on it. Your home is most likely the most important real estate you own. Your real estate can include your home where you live, commercial property where you earn income, investment property that you hope to sell for a profit, a condominium where you own specific space, and a timeshare where you have right to access property for a limited time.

How your real estate is titled, or owned, makes a big difference in how ownership to that piece of property is transferred at your death and who will become the next owner. That's why in this chapter, you have an opportunity to take stock of all your real estate and go over the ways it is, or can be, owned.

My To-Do Checklist

Done   **Need to Do**

Done	Need to Do	
☐	☐	Assemble copies of the deeds to all real estate
☐	☐	Review how your property is titled
☐	☐	Discuss your real estate ownership and taxes with a tax adviser or estate planner
☐	☐	Determine if your property qualifies for tax relief
☐	☐	Consolidate all investment and commercial property records

☐	☐	Obtain a copy of your Master Deed and condominium association documents
☐	☐	Obtain a copy of your timeshare contract
☐	☐	Complete the checklists for Chapter 7

✔ Assemble copies of the deeds to all real estate

You can tell how you own property by looking at the deed to that piece of real estate. If you do not have a copy of the deed, you can get a copy from the clerk of the land records in the county where the property is located. You will want to keep copies of each deed in your safe deposit box.

✔ Review how your property is titled

There are many different ways that you can own, or hold title, to real estate. How you hold title has a significant impact on your heirs and how your property will be distributed at your death. Take, for example, all the ways you can own your home. You can own it in your own name or jointly with others. You can keep the right to live in your home for as long as you live, even after giving ownership to someone else. You can own the space where you live but not the building. Or you can put your home into your own trust, which would then own it.

Individual Ownership

You can own real property *individually* in your own name. This means that you alone have the right to sell it, rent it, transfer it by will, and use it in any legal way. You need to state in your will who you want to inherit this property. If you do not have a will, your state's law of *intestacy* will determine who gets it. Intestacy law sets up a priority scheme of inheritance. To a degree, it tries to anticipate who the typical person would want to inherit his or her property if the property owner had gotten around to writing a will. You should check to see what your state's priority scheme is, but typically real estate would first go to a spouse, and if no spouse then to children, and if no children then to parents, then to siblings, and so forth out multiple branches of the family tree to the closest next of kin. Most intestacy laws also include rules of what to do when there are bumps in the family tree such as adopted children, deceased children with living children, or multiple marriages. Only if no next of kin can be located does the state get your property, called *escheat* to the state.

Joint Ownership

There are multiple ways you can own real estate with someone else. Your deed establishes whether you are joint owners or common owners. *Joint owners with right of survivorship* have equal ownership and rights to use and enjoy the property. When one of the joint owners dies, the surviving owner or owners automatically continue to own the property. The last surviving owner ends up as the sole owner of the property. This last owner can then leave that property by will to anyone he or she wants, or it will be distributed through intestacy rules. All joint owners must agree to sell or mortgage the property. For couples who are not married, this type of property ownership ensures that the surviving partner will automatically inherit the property. Joint owners don't have to be spouses. If they are, some states call this type of ownership *tenants by the entireties*.

Common Ownership

Ownership in common (called tenants in common) is the other primary way to own real estate with someone else. The key difference between ownership in common and joint ownership is what happens to the share of ownership when a common owner dies. Unlike joint ownership with right of survivorship, the surviving owner does not inherit any greater interest or share in the property. The common owner's share passes to the decedent's estate. Siblings who own property together, such as a beach house, may want to consider ownership in common so that each sibling's interest will pass down to their own children, rather than to the sibling or nieces and nephews. For example, Juanita and Louise as sisters share equal ownership in common of a cabin on a lake where their families frequently spend summers. Each sister has a will that states when she dies her property passes to her own children. When Juanita dies, Louise still owns half of the property, along with Juanita's kids, who own the other half.

Community Property

For spouses in nine states (Arizona, California, Idaho, Louisiana, Nevada, New Mexico, Texas, Washington, and Wisconsin), all property acquired during the marriage automatically becomes community property. The laws vary in each of these states, but the basic theory is that each spouse acquires an equal interest in the real estate. When a husband or wife dies, only half of the marital property is inheritable since the surviving spouse already owns in his or her own right half of the marital property. Each spouse has the right to assign by will the ownership of his or her portion of the community property. Property that either spouse brought into the marriage or inherits is considered separate property.

Trust Property

Another way to title property is to have it held in trust. You can read about trusts in Chapter 9. Be sure to list all trust real estate in the Trust Checklist in this chapter.

The grantor is the person who creates the trust and deeds selected real estate into the trust. Although as grantor you no longer "own" the property (your trust does), you determine who as trustee is to manage that property (it could be yourself, if you wish) and when and how the trustee is to transfer that property to the beneficiaries. The beneficiary of a trust is the person who receives the benefit of the trust. When and how assets in the trust are distributed to the beneficiary depends on the language in the trust document.

Rental Property

As a renter, you may not own where you call "home" but you still have legal rights while you live there. You could rent an apartment, have a suite in an assisted living facility, or stay in a room in a skilled nursing facility. You could also have a contract with a continuing care retirement community (CCRC), where you move from independent living to higher levels of services and care as your medical needs change, while staying within the same campus or residential community.

If you're in a senior independent living unit or a nursing home, your rights and obligations are spelled out in the rental contract, including how long you can stay, how much you pay, what services you'll get, and what you do when you want or need to move. The contracts for CCRCs can be very complicated and the fee structures are intricate. Be certain that you talk with a lawyer or a financial adviser before you sign the contract. It's a good idea to have a lawyer review any rental agreement you don't completely understand.

✔ Discuss your real estate ownership and taxes with a tax adviser or estate planner

Adjusting how property is owned is a crucial step in any estate planning. Before making changes to how you own any real property, however, you'll want to get sound advice from a professional about any tax, public benefits, or inheritance implications that you may not have thought about.

Adding a Child to a Deed

Joint ownership with right of survivorship is typically the way that spouses own their home because it is a convenient way to avoid the need to probate that property when the first spouse dies. This is because the surviving joint owner automatically becomes the sole owner on the death of the other owner. On the other hand, adding a child to a deed because you want the child to inherit your home is fraught with possible negative consequences, both to you and your child. You cannot sell your home, take out a home equity loan, or get a mortgage without your child's consent. You will not be able to get a reverse mortgage unless you and your child are both over age 62. If your child is sued, gets a divorce, or goes into bankruptcy, your jointly owned home will be involved in those legal entanglements.

By adding a child to your deed as a joint owner, you are making a gift of the value of the home, which has tax and Medicaid complications. You may need to declare the gift to the IRS by preparing gift-tax returns. Refer to IRS Publication 559 at www.irs.gov/publi cations/uac/Publication-559,-Survivors,-Executors,-and-Administrators for more details or consult with your lawyer. While it may at first sound attractive to your child that he or she is getting the house now rather than having to wait to inherit it after you die, the different tax consequences between getting it now and waiting until later may make the idea less inviting—to both of you.

When you make a gift of your home by adding your child as a joint owner, your child gets the same basis as you had at the time you make the gift. **Basis** is important in determining the amount of taxes that will be due when the house is sold. As an example, you originally purchased your home for $250,000. It has increased in value to $400,000 at the time you make the gift. You have made a gift worth $150,000. If the house is worth $500,000 when you die, your heirs get what is called stepped up basis, or the value of the house on the date of death.

Here's an example of how this would work: If your son *inherited* the home and later sells it for $600,000, he would have a basis of $500,000 and a gain of only $100,000. If your son was *gifted* the house, he would have a basis of $125,000 for the half he was gifted (half of the original basis of $250,000) and $250,000 on the half he inherited (half of the $500,000 value at date of death) for a total basis of $375,000. If he sells at $600,000 he would have a gain of $225,000. At a 15 percent capital gains rate, the difference in tax liability is $15,000 versus $33,750.

Gifting ownership of your home may also prevent or delay you from being eligible for Medicaid if you need to go into a nursing home. Medicaid rules consider that a gift made within five years of an application for Medicaid is a transfer for less than fair market value. It will assess an eligibility penalty that is calculated by dividing the value of the transfer by the state's average nursing facility private pay rate to determine how many months you have to wait before you are eligible for Medicaid. You can make gifts to your spouse without this penalty. Additionally, Medicaid does not include up to $500,000 of the value of your home in determining the maximum amount of resources you can have to be Medicaid eligible.

Keep in mind that a joint owner automatically inherits any jointly owned property upon your death. This can be one of the useful ways to pass property on to another without the delay or hassle of probate. What you say in your will about who is to inherit your property does not affect what you have said in a deed about who you want to inherit that property. The deed rules over the will.

Note: Medicaid eligibility rules frequently change and vary from state to state. Check with a lawyer experienced with your state's Medicaid rules before making any gift.

Life Estate

By creating a life estate, you can transfer the ownership of your home to another person but reserve the right to continue to live in the home until you die. Upon your death, the other person automatically gets the right to take possession. For example, Tom and Mary together own their home and want to remain there until the last one dies. They can create a joint life estate with their children as the remaindermen. Tom and Mary can live at home until the last spouse dies; then the kids own the whole property. As a life tenant, you continue to be responsible for the taxes, insurance, and maintenance of the property, but you avoid some of the adverse consequences of jointly owning property with your children.

✔ Determine if your property qualifies for tax relief

Depending on where you live, you may be eligible for property tax relief on your residence. Most states or counties offer some reduction in taxes based on the age, income, disability, or military status of the homeowner. To find out if you are eligible, you can contact your local agency where you pay taxes, your state department of revenue or taxation, or your local area agency on aging. Check out the Lincoln Institute of Land Policy to find out what special tax policies are available in your state at www.lincolninst.edu/subcenters/significant-features-property-tax/Report_Residential_ Property_Tax_Relief_Programs.aspx.

✔ Consolidate all investment and commercial property records

You may have a second home where you spend part of the year, land that you inherited and share with other relatives, investment property that you rent out, or a farm operation that you run. As with any income-producing asset, you should maintain in logical order any records relating to the management of your investment or farm property. These records could include all business plans, land or equipment leases, rental income, easements, assessments, insurance policies, tax records, accounts payable, and inventory of all equipment.

In addition to the deeds to any business or commercial property that you own, you should organize all the other documents that someone would need to locate should he or she have to take over management of the property tomorrow. At a minimum, you should consolidate your business plan, contracts, lease agreements, account records, bank statements, and tax records for each property.

✔ Obtain a copy of your Master Deed and condominium association documents

A condominium is a special form of ownership. Typically a condominium owner individually owns a specific unit as well as jointly owns with all the other unit owners the common areas such as the public hallways, lobby, grounds, and recreational areas. You should have a copy of the Master Deed or Declaration, which describes the space that you own, the common areas, and any restrictions on how you can use or modify your unit or the common areas. A copy of the Master Deed that you signed should be on file in your local court house.

You should also have a copy of your condominium association documents. The condominium association includes all the unit owners who manage the condominium through an elected board of directors. Your condominium association may also have a separate set of bylaws and/or rules that further set out how the condominium is to be managed, pet restrictions, color choices, and how monthly unit fees are assessed, among other details.

✔ Obtain a copy of your timeshare contract

A timeshare is a way to own the right to use property, rather than direct ownership of the property. With most timeshares, multiple people have the right to use the same property, with each having a specific period of time when they have exclusive use of the property. You may purchase a specific week in a specific unit or be able to negotiate a rotating time schedule or trade your share for use of multiple properties. Because there are so many variations on the timeshare concept, your contract is very important. It will explain to you and your family what happens to the timeshare on your death.

Real Estate Action Checklists

The checklists in Chapter 7 are set out in the following order:

- *Business*
- *Condominium*
- *Farm Land*
- *Investment*
- *Primary Residence*
- *Rental Residence*
- *Secondary Residence*
- *Timeshare*
- *Trust*
- *Real Estate: Other*

Business

- ☐ I do not own any business property.
- ☐ I own the following business property:

Property address:_____

Township: _____ County: _____

My ownership interest is:

- ☐ Sole
- ☐ Community property
- ☐ Joint with right of survivorship
- ☐ Tenant in common
- ☐ In trust

With:

_____

_____

Purchase price: _____

- ☐ I do not owe any money on the property.
- ☐ I owe money on the property as follows:

Financial institution/Loan servicer: _____

Phone: _____ Fax: _____

Address: _____

_____

Email: _____ Website: _____

Balance due: _____ Monthly payment: _____

Property address:_____

Township: _____ County: _____

My ownership interest is:

- ☐ Sole
- ☐ Community property
- ☐ Joint with right of survivorship
- ☐ Tenant in common
- ☐ In trust

With:

_____

_____

Purchase price: _____

    ☐   I do not owe any money on the property.

    ☐   I owe money on the property as follows:

Financial institution/Loan servicer: _____

Phone: _____ Fax: _____

Address: _____

_____

Email: _____ Website: _____

Balance due: _____ Monthly payment: _____

Condominium

☐ I do not own any condominium property.

☐ I own the following condominium property:

Property address:_____

_____

Township: _____ County: _____

Condominium association contact:

Name: _____

Phone: _____ Fax: _____

Address: _____

_____

Email: _____

My condominium association dues are:

_____

Purchase price: _____

☐ I do not owe any money on the condominium.

☐ I owe money on the condominium as follows:

Financial institution/Loan servicer: _____

Phone: _____ Fax: _____

Address: _____

_____

Email: _____ Website: _____

Type of Mortgage:_____

Balance due: _____ Monthly payment: _____

Farm Land

- ☐ I do not own any farm land.
- ☐ I own the following farm land:

Property address:_____

_____

Township: _____ County: _____

My ownership interest is:

- ☐ Sole
- ☐ Community property
- ☐ Joint with right of survivorship
- ☐ Tenant in common
- ☐ In trust
- ☐ Life estate

With:

_____

_____

Purchase price: _____

- ☐ I do not owe any money on the farm land.
- ☐ I owe money on the farm land as follows:

Financial institution/Loan servicer: _____

Phone: _____ Fax: _____

Address: _____

_____

Email: _____ Website: _____

Type of loan: _____

Balance due: _____ Monthly payment: _____

Investment

- ☐ I do not own any investment property.
- ☐ I own the following investment property:

Property address:_____

_____

Township: _____

County: _____

My ownership interest is:

- ☐ Sole
- ☐ Community property
- ☐ Joint with right of survivorship
- ☐ Tenant in common
- ☐ In trust
- ☐ Life estate

With: _____

_____

Purchase price: _____

- ☐ I do not owe any money on the real estate.
- ☐ I owe money on the real estate as follows:

Financial institution/Mortgage servicer:_____

Phone: _____ Fax: _____

Address: _____

_____

Email: _____ Website: _____

Type of loan:_____

Balance due: _____ Monthly payment: _____

Primary Residence

☐ I do not own a residence.

☐ I own the following residence:

Property address:_____

_____

Township: _____

County: _____

My ownership interest is:

☐ Sole

☐ Community property

☐ Joint with right of survivorship

☐ Tenant in common

☐ In trust

☐ Life estate

With: _____

_____

Purchase price: _____

☐ I do not owe any money on my residence.

☐ I owe money on my residence as follows:

Financial institution/Mortgage servicer:_____

Phone: _____ Fax: _____

Address: _____

_____

Email: _____ Website: _____

Type of mortgage:_____

Balance due: _____ Monthly payment: _____

Rental Residence

☐ I do not rent the living space where I live.

☐ I live in the following rental property:

Property address:_____

_____

Unit: _____

Property manager:

Name: _____

Phone: _____ Fax: _____

Address: _____

_____

Email: _____ Website: _____

I can stay here until: _____

Monthly payments: _____

Additional payments for services: _____

Secondary Residence

☐ I do not own a secondary residence.

☐ I own the following secondary residence:

Property address:_____

_____

Township: _____ County: _____

My ownership interest is:

☐ Sole

☐ Community property

☐ Joint with right of survivorship

☐ Tenant in common

☐ In trust

☐ Life estate

With: _____

_____

Purchase price: _____

☐ I do not owe any money on my secondary residence.

☐ I owe money on my secondary residence as follows:

Financial institution/Mortgage servicer:_____

Phone: _____ Fax: _____

Address: _____

_____

Email: _____ Website: _____

Type of mortgage:_____

Balance due: _____ Monthly payment: _____

Timeshare

☐   I do not own any timeshare property.

☐   I own the following timeshare property:

Timeshare management company contact: _____

Phone: _____ Fax: _____

Address: _____

_____

Email: _____ Website: _____

Type share: _____ Purchase price: _____

☐   I do not owe any money on the timeshare.

☐   I owe money on the timeshare as follows:

Financial institution/Mortgage servicer: _____

Phone: _____ Fax: _____

Address: _____

_____

Email: _____ Website: _____

Type of mortgage: _____

Balance due: _____ Monthly payment: _____

My annual maintenance fee is $ _____ It is due on _____

It is due to:

Name: _____

Phone: _____ Fax: _____

Address: _____

_____

Email: _____

Trust

- ☐ I am not the grantor or beneficiary of any property held in trust.
- ☐ I am the grantor of the following property held in trust:
- ☐ I am the primary beneficiary of the following property held in trust:
- ☐ I am the secondary beneficiary of the following property held in trust:

Property address:_____

_____

Township: _____ County: _____

Grantor: _____

Trustee: _____

Primary beneficiary/beneficiaries: _____

Secondary beneficiary/beneficiaries: _____

- ☐ I am the grantor of the following property held in trust:
- ☐ I am the primary beneficiary of the following property held in trust:
- ☐ I am the secondary beneficiary of the following property held in trust

Property address:_____

_____

Township: _____ County: _____

Grantor: _____

Trustee: _____

Primary beneficiary/beneficiaries: _____

Secondary beneficiary/beneficiaries: _____

Real Estate: Other

The following miscellaneous information about my real estate may be of interest:

_____

_____

_____

_____

_____

_____

_____

_____

_____

_____

_____

_____

_____

_____

_____

_____

_____

_____

_____

_____

_____

_____

_____

_____

_____

_____

_____

_____

CHAPTER 8
OTHER ASSETS AND DEBTS

Always do right. This will gratify some and astonish the rest.

—Mark Twain

The preceding chapters provided checklists for you to record your checking and savings accounts, insurance, investments, and real estate. This chapter is included to provide you with pages to list your various other assets and debts. Take the time to think about all the personal assets you have, whether priceless heirlooms, irreplaceable family photographs, a special collection of model trains, Beatles posters, or shot glasses. You don't need to note every asset you own, as the listing could go on for pages. These checklists are where you can record significant special possessions.

Here you can also note your virtual assets. Your iTunes, Shutterfly, Snapfish, ebooks, airline and hotel rewards programs, as well as your Facebook, Twitter, and other social media sites have "value," even if not in a strictly monetary sense. Be kind to your family and let them know what types of accounts or assets you have online and how to access them when you can't.

You will also find checklists for your financial obligations such as credit cards, money you have borrowed from others, and other types of debts that your family needs to know about. Sad but true, your creditors will need to be paid before your family members will be able to receive their inheritance.

My To-Do Checklist

Done	Need to Do	
☐	☐	Assemble receipts or appraisals for higher-valued possessions
☐	☐	Photograph or videotape special possessions
☐	☐	Write down stories about how you acquired special possessions
☐	☐	Label the photographs
☐	☐	Inventory your digital assets
☐	☐	Put the terms of any personals loans in writing
☐	☐	List contact information for credit cards
☐	☐	Note if you have a reverse mortgage
☐	☐	Complete the checklists for Chapter 8

Because checklists cannot be tailor-made to cover all the things everyone might have, this chapter provides places to list a number of common assets—motor vehicles, frequent flyer miles, and online accounts as well as names and addresses of people to whom you owe money, business interests you own, and information regarding any claims or lawsuits you may have against other persons—or they against you.

Use these checklists to record information about any of these possible assets. You may be surprised at what you have. Information about these not-so-obvious assets will be invaluable to your family. Executors don't like surprises when it comes time to finalizing an estate. This information can help avoid surprises. It may also save your executor time and your estate money when having to compile the inventory of your estate.

✔ Assemble receipts or appraisals for higher-valued possessions

Additional space is provided for you to list any assets of value you may own. Make sure that you list any furniture, paintings and artwork, coin or stamp collections, jewelry, and musical instruments that have great value. You don't need to list everything, but do include items of special interest or value. Receipts or appraisals are important in establishing the value of your special possessions.

✔ Photograph or videotape special possessions

Now is a good time to inventory your special possessions. One way to do this is to take photographs or even make a video as you walk through your rooms, closets, cabinets, attic, garage, and basement. After you have documented what you have, put the disk with the digital pictures or the video tape in your safe deposit box or other fireproof storage or in cloud storage, indicating where it is stored. This documentation will be invaluable not only to your executor, but having these pictures also will make it much easier to file an insurance claim for loss or theft or to prepare an estate inventory.

✔ Write down stories about how you acquired special possessions

After you have taken the photos, go the extra step to tell any interesting stories about how you acquired special items. You could talk into a tape recorder, make notes by hand or on the computer, or dictate the stories to a family member. Only you will be able to pass on the history of the silver bowl you got as a wedding present from Aunt Tully or how you haggled with a street merchant for the painting in the dining room. Be sure your family knows that the opal ring came from your maternal grandmother, while the pocket watch was Great Uncle Randolph's.

✔ Label the photographs

Years from now your grandkids won't remember if the family photograph hanging on the bedroom wall is from your mother's side of the family or your spouse's. A note you put on the back of the frame that says when and where the picture was taken and who's in the picture will be greatly appreciated. If you are not sure, check with others who might help you to get the facts captured now. The next generation will have an even harder time tracking the information down.

The same advice applies to those boxes and albums where you have stored family photographs. You'll have fun and raise some fond memories as you go through to label who's in the pictures and where they were taken. If you can't identify who's in the picture, you can be sure your kids won't have a clue. I've just gone through a cedar chest full of my in-laws' framed family photos. For too many of them, I wish I knew more about the family stories behind the pictures.

✔ Inventory your digital assets

Be sure not to overlook the Digital Assets Checklist and the Rewards Programs Checklist in this chapter. In this digital age, user IDs and their associated passwords are essential to gain access to email, electronic banking, online bill paying, bitcoins, iTunes files, e-books, games, Facebook, LinkedIn, Twitter, PayPal, blog posts, movies, videos, digital photo storage, and shopping sites, to name just some of the most obvious. You may have a username and password to access your benefit information at MyMedicare.gov and My SocialSecurity.gov, or a TreasuryDirect account. Many of our business and personal records and files are found or stored online.

Have you ever thought about what would happen to all that information if you suddenly become unable to use your computer or when you die? Most websites and social media, as well as federal and state privacy and computer fraud laws, make it very difficult for anyone other than you to have access to your digital accounts and records. You probably want those protections now, too, but in an emergency or after death, they can be huge barriers to your family or those you want to have access. Most current laws now criminalize, or at least penalize, unauthorized access of computers and digital accounts. Many digital providers are prohibited from disclosing most account information to anyone without the account holder's consent. And most sites aren't very clear, or are silent, about how you might go about giving consent to someone else to have access.

You can, in your durable power of attorney or will, authorize your agent or your executor to have access to your online accounts. You may want to prepare a special power of attorney just to give someone authority to manage your digital accounts. Of course, if there are certain accounts you don't want anyone else to access, put that in your document, too. States are just now beginning to write laws about what happens to digital assets on the incapacity or death of the owner. Read the privacy or access policies of key websites to learn what they allow. Each site may have different procedures and steps you need to take.

Be sure to have a secure list of your online accounts with usernames and passwords. Without that, your family will waste many hours trying to figure out basic information, such as if your utility bill is on automatic bill payment, or if your credit card bill has been paid, or even how to unlock your computer or smartphone.

A word of caution: As valuable as this information is going to be to your family, it is a gold mine for identity thieves! Keep this checklist in a very secure place. You may want to tell just one or two trusted family members where it is located. But also remember that you need to keep it up to date. We all need to change our passwords frequently to keep them secure. This means you may want to enter the information in pencil so it can be easily changed, or keep a secure electronic file that you can update.

✔ Put the terms of any personal loans in writing

Your family may have little knowledge of your debts. While you do not need to list fluctuating monthly bills, note in the checklist if you have borrowed money from or lent money to a relative, friend, or associate.

All personal loans should be in writing so both you and your borrower know the terms for paying back the money. If you intend to forgive any debts at your death, be sure to put your intentions in writing. Forgiving a loan becomes a gift, which can have consequences in settling your estate, determining taxes, and being eligible for Medicaid.

✔ List contact information for credit cards

It's important that you have a list of all your credit card accounts. You need to have this list readily available now in case you need to report that a card has been lost or stolen. Later, your family members need this information so they will know what companies to contact after your death to close the account. The credit card companies, as well as the credit reporting bureaus, need to know to flag the account with a note that the owner is deceased. Sad as it may sound, identity thieves are known to read obituaries to seek potential victims. They'll try to use any still open credit card accounts of a dead person as long as they can get away with their thievery. They may also try to open new accounts knowing that a dead person doesn't check credit reports or open mail.

✔ Note if you have a reverse mortgage

A reverse mortgage is a loan against your home that requires no repayment for as long as you live there. It is offered by the U.S. Federal Housing Administration to homeowners aged 62 or older. These federally insured and regulated loans are called Home Equity Conversion Mortgages or HECMs. A reverse mortgage is different from other types of loans because the borrower does not make payments during the loan.

A reverse mortgage is one option for you to consider if you want to use the equity in your home to help meet your daily living or medical expenses, but do your research because there are risks.

You can select whether you want to receive the loan proceeds as a lump sum or as monthly disbursements. Depending on your circumstances and needs, a reverse mortgage may allow you to stay financially secure in your home because you don't have to worry about a mortgage payment.

If you are eligible, you can get a reverse mortgage, like a traditional mortgage, from a private lender (such as a bank) that is secured by the equity in your house. Unlike a traditional mortgage that gets smaller as loan payments are made, however, the reverse mortgage typically gets larger over time. The reason the mortgage gets larger is that compound interest on the amount borrowed continues to increase the longer the loan is in place. You do not need to make payments until you die, move, or sell your home. Then the entire loan must be paid back. This usually means that the home must be sold instead of being passed on to your family.

Why is this? If your increasing loan balance grows so it equals or exceeds the value of your home, then your total debt is limited to your home's value, if your home is sold to repay the loan. If your family wishes to keep the home after you die or you move and pay off the loan with other proceeds, such as a new mortgage, you or your estate must pay the full loan balance.

Because reverse mortgages are quite different from any other loan, you need to do your homework carefully and thoroughly before considering one. As a protection to you so you understand all the consequences and benefits of a reverse mortgage, you must receive independent counseling by a certified counselor before the lender can issue the loan. You can find a list of certified HECM counselors at www.hud.gov/offices/hsg/sfh/hecm/hecm list.cfm.

While the benefits of using your home's equity to meet expenses can be substantial, the upfront and ongoing costs involved in a reverse mortgage are high. These fees, including an origination fee, mortgage insurance premium, closing costs, and loan servicing fees, can amount to thousands of dollars. Unless you are facing a financial emergency, you may want to consider other options before taking out a reverse mortgage. Your family needs to know if you have a reverse mortgage on your home and realize that the loan must be repaid as soon as you die, move, or sell your home.

Other Assets and Debts
Action Checklists

The checklists in Chapter 8 are set out in the following order:

- *Business Interests*
- *Collectibles*
- *Copyrights, Patents, and Royalties*
- *Credit/Debit Cards*
- *Digital Assets*
- *Lawsuits and Judgments*
- *Outstanding Loans*
- *Personal Debts*
- *Personal Property*
- *Reverse Mortgage*
- *Rewards Programs*
- *Storage Units*
- *Vehicles*
- *Assets and Debts: Other*

Business Interests

☐   I do not have any business interests.

☐   I have the following business interests:

Business name: _____

Type of business:_____

Corporation: _____

Partners: _____

% of ownership: _____

Phone: _____ Fax: _____

Address: _____

_____

Website:_____

Business name: _____

Type of business:_____

Corporation: _____

Partners: _____

% of ownership: _____

Phone: _____ Fax: _____

Address: _____

_____

Website:_____

My business documents are located:_____

_____

Collectibles

☐ I do not own any collectibles.

☐ I own the following collectibles:

Type: _____

Description: _____

Value: _____

Type: _____

Description: _____

Value: _____

Type: _____

Description: _____

Valuc: _____

Type: _____

Description: _____

Value: _____

Type: _____

Description: _____

Value: _____

Type: _____

Description: _____

Value: _____

Type: _____

Description: _____

Value: _____

Appraisals are located: _____

My letter of instruction that explains who is to receive these collectibles is located:

_____

Copyrights, Patents, and Royalties

☐   I do not have any copyrights or patents.

☐   I have the following copyrights or patents:

Description: _____

Date granted:_____ Termination date: _____

Status: _____

Copyright or patent #: _____

Description: _____

Date granted:_____ Termination date: _____

Status: _____

Copyright or patent #: _____

****

☐   I do not have any royalty agreements.

☐   I have the following royalty agreements:

Description: _____

Date granted:_____ Termination date: _____

Status: _____

Royalty amount: _____

Description: _____

Date granted:_____ Termination date: _____

Status: _____

Royalty amount: _____

Credit/Debit Cards

☐ I do not have any credit or debit cards.

☐ I have the following credit or debit cards:

Name of credit/debit card: _____

Contact phone: _____

Website: _____

Account number: _____

Debit card PIN: _____

Amount due: _____

Name(s) on account: _____

Name of credit/debit card: _____

Contact phone: _____

Website: _____

Account number: _____

Debit card PIN: _____

Amount due: _____

Name(s) on account: _____

Name of credit/debit card: _____

Contact phone: _____

Website: _____

Account number: _____

Debit card PIN: _____

Amount due: _____

Name(s) on account: _____

Name of credit/debit card: _____

Contact phone: _____

Website: _____

Account number: _____

Debit card PIN: _____

Amount due: _____

Name(s) on account: _____

Name of credit/debit card: _____

Contact phone: _____

Website: _____

Account number: _____

Debit card PIN: _____

Amount due: _____

Name(s) on account: _____

Name of credit/debit card: _____

Contact phone: _____

Website: _____

Account number: _____

Debit card PIN: _____

Amount due: _____

Name(s) on account: _____

My username and passwords for online access are located: _____

Digital Assets

Be sure to include all of your digital or online accounts, such as online banking; online credit and debit card accounts; retail shopping sites; cloud storage for photos, videos, and music; social media such as Twitter and Facebook; and MyMedicare and MySocialSecurity. Record your airline, hotel, and rental car loyalty rewards programs on the Rewards Programs Checklist in this chapter.

Word of caution: Carefully secure this list of passwords!

☐ I have designated _____ to serve as my fiduciary or agent to have access to my digital assets.

☐ I have the following usernames and passwords:

Website:_____

Username:_____ Password: _____

Website:_____

Username:_____ Password: _____

Website:_____

Use name:_____ Password: _____

Website:_____

Username:_____ Password: _____

Website:_____

Username:_____ Password: _____

Website:_____

Username:_____ Password: _____

Website:_____

Username:_____ Password: _____

Website:_____

Username:_____ Password: _____

Website:_____

Username:_____ Password: _____

Website:_____

Username:_____ Password: _____

Website:_____

Username:_____ Password: _____

Website:_____

Username:_____ Password: _____

Website:_____

Username:_____ Password: _____

Website:_____

Username:_____ Password: _____

Website:_____

Username:_____ Password: _____

Website:_____

Username:_____ Password: _____

Website:_____

Username:_____ Password: _____

My security questions and answers are located: _____

Lawsuits and Judgments

☐ I do not have any lawsuits or legal claims pending.

☐ I have the following lawsuits or legal claims pending:

Case name: _____

Court: _____

Attorney: _____

Type lawsuit or legal claim: _____

Case name: _____

Court: _____

Attorney: _____

Type lawsuit or legal claim: _____

****

☐ I do not have any uncollected legal judgments pending.

☐ I have the following uncollected legal judgments pending:

Case name: _____

Court: _____

Attorney: _____

Type of judgment: _____

Case name: _____

Court: _____

Attorney: _____

Type of judgment: _____

Outstanding Loans

☐   No one owes me money.

☐   The following people owe me money:

Name of borrower: _____

Contact phone: _____

Address: _____

_____

Amount due: _____

Name of borrower: _____

Contact phone: _____

Address: _____

_____

Amount due: _____

Name of borrower: _____

Contact phone: _____

Address: _____

_____

Amount due: _____

Name of borrower: _____

Contact phone: _____

Address: _____

_____

Amount due: _____

Personal Debts

☐ I do not owe anyone any money.

☐ I owe the following people or entities money:

Internal Revenue Service: _____

Contact phone: _____

Address: _____

_____

Amount due: _____

State Department of Taxation: _____

Contact phone: _____

Address: _____

_____

Amount due: _____

Name of lender: _____

Contact phone: _____

Address: _____

_____

Amount due: _____

Name of lender: _____

Contact phone: _____

Address: _____

_____

Amount due: _____

Name of lender: _____

Contact phone: _____

Address: _____

_____

Amount due: _____

Name of lender: _____

Contact phone: _____

Address: _____

_____

Amount due: _____

Name of lender: _____

Contact phone: _____

Address: _____

_____

Amount due: _____

Name of lender: _____

Contact phone: _____

Address: _____

_____

Amount due: _____

Name of lender: _____

Contact phone: _____

Address: _____

_____

Amount due: _____

Personal Property

☐ I do not have any personal property.

☐ I have the following special possessions, including antiques, jewelry, art, furniture, silver, and musical instruments:

Item description: _____

Value: _____ Location: _____

Item description: _____

Value: _____ Location: _____

Item description: _____

Value: _____ Location: _____

Item description: _____

Value: _____ Location: _____

Item description: _____

Value: _____ Location: _____

Item description: _____

Value: _____ Location: _____

Item description: _____

Value: _____ Location: _____

Item description: _____

Value: _____ Location: _____

Item description: _____

Value: _____ Location: _____

Item description: _____

Value: _____ Location: _____

Item description: _____

Value: _____ Location: _____

Item description: _____

Value: _____ Location: _____

Item description: _____

Value: _____ Location: _____

Item description: _____

Value: _____ Location: _____

Item description: _____

Value: _____ Location: _____

Item description: _____

Value: _____ Location: _____

Item description: _____

Value: _____ Location: _____

Item description: _____

Value: _____ Location: _____

My letter of instruction on how and to whom these personal items are to be distributed is located: _____

Photos or videos of these personal items are located: _____

Reverse Mortgage

☐ I do not have a reverse mortgage.

☐ I do have the following reverse mortgage:

Property address:_____

_____

Township: _____ County: _____

Financial institution: _____

Phone: _____ Fax: _____

Address: _____

_____

Email: _____ Website: _____

Type of reverse mortgage:_____

Mortgage account #. _____

Rewards Programs

☐   I do not have any frequent flier mileage accounts.

☐   I have frequent flier mileage with the following airlines:

Airline: _____

Website: _____

Frequent flyer #: _____

Username: _____ Password/PIN: _____

Airline: _____

Website: _____

Frequent flyer #: _____

Username: _____ Password/PIN: _____

Airline: _____

Website: _____

Frequent flyer #: _____

Username: _____ Password/PIN: _____

Airline: _____

Website: _____

Frequent flyer #: _____

Username: _____ Password/PIN: _____

Airline: _____

Website: _____

Frequent flyer #: _____

Username: _____ Password/PIN: _____

☐ I do not have any hotel loyalty rewards programs.

☐ I have loyalty rewards with the following hotel companies:

Hotel: _____

Website: _____

Rewards #: _____

Username: _____ Password/PIN: _____

Hotel: _____

Website: _____

Rewards #: _____

Username: _____ Password/PIN: _____

Hotel: _____

Website: _____

Rewards #: _____

Username: _____ Password/PIN: _____

☐ I do not have any rental car company loyalty rewards programs.

☐ I have loyalty rewards with the following rental car companies:

Rental company: _____

Website: _____

Rewards #: _____

Username: _____ Password/PIN: _____

Rental company: _____

Website: _____

Rewards #: _____

Username: _____ Password/PIN: _____

Storage Units

☐   I do not have any items in public storage.

☐   I have the following items in public storage:

Storage company: _____

Address: _____

Unit #: _____

Website: _____

Username: _____ Password/PIN: _____

Monthly rent: _____ Autopay: ☐ Yes   ☐ No

Storage company: _____

Address: _____

Unit #: _____

Website: _____

Username: _____ Password/PIN: _____

Monthly rent: _____ Autopay: ☐ Yes   ☐ No

Storage company: _____

Address: _____

Unit #: _____

Website: _____

Username: _____ Password/PIN: _____

Monthly rent: _____ Autopay: ☐ Yes   ☐ No

Storage company: _____

Address: _____

Unit #: _____

Website: _____

Username: _____ Password/PIN: _____

Monthly rent: _____ Autopay: ☐ Yes   ☐ No

The key or lock combination is located: _____

Vehicles

☐ I do not own any vehicles, including cars, trucks, recreational vehicles, boats, and campers.

☐ I own the following vehicles:

Make: _____ Model: _____

Year: _____ Tag #: _____

Title is located: _____

Make: _____ Model: _____

Year: _____ Tag #: _____

Title is located: _____

Make: _____ Model: _____

Year: _____ Tag #: _____

Title is located: _____

Make: _____ Model: _____

Year: _____ Tag #: _____

Title is located: _____

Make: _____ Model: _____

Year: _____ Tag #: _____

Title is located: _____

Make: _____ Model: _____

Year: _____ Tag #: _____

Title is located: _____

Make: _____ Model: _____

Year: _____ Tag #: _____

Title is located: _____

Assets and Debts: Other

The following miscellaneous information about my assets or debts may be of interest:

_____

_____

_____

_____

_____

_____

_____

_____

_____

_____

_____

_____

_____

_____

_____

_____

_____

_____

_____

_____

_____

_____

_____

_____

_____

_____

CHAPTER 9
WILLS, TRUSTS, AND POWERS OF ATTORNEY

It matters not how strait the gate,
How charged with punishments the scroll.
I am the master of my fate:
I am the captain of my soul.

—*William Ernest Henley*

To complete your advance planning, you should have in place various legal documents that set out your wishes for how you want your estate distributed after your death. (Many people think an "estate" is just for someone with mansions, fancy cars, and lots of money. But anyone with a home, bank account, retirement savings, or even a set of china or a car has an estate.) A last will and testament—or more simply, a will—is the primary document to lay out who you want to receive your legacy. A codicil is used to amend your will when circumstances change your plan. A living trust, in special circumstances, can be used as a companion to your will in directing how you want your property managed and distributed. In addition to these estate documents, you'll also want to consider a financial power of attorney to make sure that if you are disabled, your estate is in good hands.

To get these documents done right, you'll first want to talk with experts in estate planning and taxes. This chapter walks you through the process and provides you with an opportunity to review the documents you have (or need) and indicate where your family can find them.

My To-Do Checklist

Done   Need to Do

Done	Need to Do	
☐	☐	Consult with an estate planning expert
☐	☐	Consult with a tax adviser
☐	☐	Document any major financial gifts
☐	☐	Identify a source of funding for costs to close the estate
☐	☐	Prepare or review your will
☐	☐	Prepare any necessary codicils to your will
☐	☐	Consider if a living trust should be part of your estate plan
☐	☐	Select an agent to manage your financial affairs
☐	☐	Prepare a letter of instruction
☐	☐	Discuss your plan with those who need to know
☐	☐	Complete the checklists for Chapter 9

✔ Consult with an estate planning expert

As you begin considering the legal documents you will need, you'll probably want to consult with an estate planning expert who can guide you through the process. To ease you in, here's a cheat sheet on the basics you'll learn.

Your financial affairs will have to be settled by someone no matter how much planning you have done—or not done. The first step to setting your financial affairs at your death is for someone to identify everything you own, including bank accounts, investments, personal property, and real estate, and everything you owe, such as mortgages, debts, medical bills, and funeral expenses. Then all your assets have to be categorized by those assets that are in your probate estate or those distributed outside of probate. Also your taxable assets, if any, have to be calculated. If you've filled out all the checklists in the previous chapters, bring those to the estate planner. The more work you have done ahead of time in listing what you have, the less time and effort your family will have to expend in settling your financial affairs.

Types of Estates

What you own at the time of your death can be grouped into different categories depending on various factors. Your "estate" is everything that you own at the time of your death. Your ***probate estate*** includes those things that will be distributed according to your will or your state's law of probate distribution. Then there's your ***taxable estate***, which includes those assets that the federal government or your state can tax. You could also have a ***trust estate***, which is anything you have deeded to a trust (more on that later in this chapter). As you do estate planning, you need to appreciate the differences. Not everything in your estate is part of your probate estate, and not everything in your estate is subject to taxes.

It may sound like an oxymoron, but your probate estate includes everything that you have previously determined is *not* part of your probate estate. You take something out of your probate estate by owning property jointly with right of survivorship; by transferring property into a trust; and by indicating a beneficiary of your life insurance, annuity, investment account, or retirement fund. What is remaining is your probate estate. Your probate estate will be distributed according to the directions in your will or, if you have no will, according to the distribution laws in your state. If you have a will, you die *testate*; without a will you are said to have died *intestate*.

Probate

Probate is the court procedure that determines the validity of your will (if any), determines who will be in charge of settling your affairs, identifies your heirs, inventories your probate assets, determines claims against your estate, calculates any taxes to be paid, and makes sure the remaining proceeds are distributed to the proper persons. In your will, you establish who gets what and how much. If you don't have a will, your state's intestacy law does that for you. In effect, the probate court makes sure that your wishes are carried out, supervises how your estate is distributed, adjudicates any disputes over the terms of your will or claims against your estate, and sorts out family disagreements.

✔ Consult with a tax adviser

You'll also want to consult a tax adviser as you think through your estate plan and prepare your documentation. Even if your taxable estate is well below the federal estate tax exclusion ($5.35 million in 2014), there may be tax consequences to you and your heirs that you'll need to consider. One example, discussed in Chapter 7, is the difference in the basis for property that is gifted or inherited. Your tax adviser also can review your major financial gifts and work with you on a gifting plan if you need to reduce the size of your taxable estate.

✔ Document any major financial gifts

The IRS considers any gift to be taxable to you unless it falls within four specific exceptions.

- You can make gifts of any amount to your spouse without gift tax consequences.
- You can make a gift of tuition or medical expenses for another if you pay the money directly to the institution or provider.
- You can make annual gifts of less than the amount set by the IRS. For gifts made in 2014, that limit is $14,000.

- You can make gifts to political organizations and qualifying charities.

All other gifts for less than the item's fair market value should be reported to the IRS in the year you make the gift. Your executor will need documentation of any gifts you have made during your lifetime to be able to calculate if any estate tax is due. The IRS considers the laws on gift taxes to be among the most complex in the tax code, so to avoid tax surprises, seek professional advice before you make the gift.

Gifts can also complicate your eligibility for Medicaid. Medicaid is another very complex area, primarily because the laws frequently change and the details can vary from state to state. To simply summarize current law, before you can be eligible for Medicaid assistance in paying for your medical care in a long-term care facility, you will have to demonstrate your need. Part of that assessment looks at gifts ("transfers for less than fair market value") in the five years prior to your application for Medicaid. As with the gift tax laws, there are permissible ways to make gifts under Medicaid rules, but they are similarly complex.

Tax and Medicaid laws change frequently, so check with a tax adviser or an estate planning elder law attorney for current tax and Medicaid provisions before you make any substantial gift.

✔ Identify a source of funding for costs to close the estate

Much has been written about the cost of probate, with some suggesting that probate is a detrimental process that should be avoided at all costs. In reality, going through probate means simply settling your estate. Settling your estate does incur fees and costs that cannot be avoided, but you can control some of the expense through advance preparation and planning. Some minor costs of the probate process include filing fees to open the probate case by presenting your will and publishing legal notices in newspapers. Some states may also charge other filing fees for the inventory or accountings.

The major expenses in settling your estate—with or without probate court involvement—are professional fees for an attorney, real estate agent, appraiser, accountant, or tax preparer. The attorney for your estate advises your personal representative (the executor of your will or administrator of your estate), assists in filing court documents, and represents your estate in any disputes. These professional fees will be paid as an expense of your estate. The more complex your financial affairs are, the higher the professional fees will be. Also the less clear your wishes, the higher the professional fees.

The other major expense in settling your estate is compensation for your personal representative. Depending on the laws of your state, your personal representative will be paid a percentage of the inventory value of your estate or a set fee determined by the judge. States that use a percentage to calculate the fee typically use a sliding scale. As the size of the estate increases, a smaller percentage is taken from the greater portions of the estate. For example, a personal representative might be entitled to a fee of 5 percent on the first $10,000 of an estate, 4 percent of the next $25,000, 3 percent of the next $50,000, and 2 percent of anything over $85,000.

In the other states, the personal representative's fee is based on what would be "just and reasonable" compensation for the amount of work the representative has to do. The amount of work involved by two personal representatives can differ considerably even for estates of the same value. It is much simpler to administer an estate if assets can be readily found, no claims against the estate need to be resolved, and no family squabbles need to be negotiated. You can make your personal representative's job much easier—and less expensive to your estate—by completing the checklists in this book. The more advance work you do, the less time and expense your personal representative has to incur. Of course, you can say in your will that your executor is not to be paid, but before adding that provision, think about all the work he or she will need to do.

✔ Prepare or review your will

A will, or last will and testament, is the legal document by which you determine who you want to receive your probate property. If you have a friend, domestic partner, or significant other who is not related to you that you want to receive any of your estate, you must have a will. By having a will you can also make sure that someone (other than your spouse) who would inherit if you don't have a will does not.

In your will, you also set out what you want your beneficiaries to receive. You can make gifts in your will of specific items, such as your car or wedding ring; or a set dollar amount; or percentages divided among several friends or family members. Another way to establish who is to get some of your personal property is to make a list, or letter of instruction, that is separate from your will; this is explained later in this chapter.

Your will can also indicate donations to the charities, schools, or religious groups you support, letting you take advantage of tax laws that encourage private philanthropy.

In your will, you name the person you want to be in charge of managing your estate, and the court will appoint that person as your *executor*. If you have not nominated an executor in your will, the court will appoint an *administrator* for you. The duties of your *personal representative*, whether called an executor or administrator, are the same.

You should choose your personal representative with care because that person has many responsibilities. It can be a big task that requires good financial skills, attention to detail, patience, and probably a dose of diplomacy. Your personal representative must inventory your assets, have them appraised, pay bills, publish legal notices, prepare your final income tax return, work with financial institutions to close out accounts, record documents to sell or transfer real estate, find and notify beneficiaries, file any estate tax returns, and file inventories and accountings with the court. All the while your personal representative must keep happy the anxious and impatient debtors and beneficiaries of your estate.

If you have minor children, you need to name who you want to be their guardian until they reach the age of majority. If you wish to leave assets to any minors, you'll want to create a testamentary trust so their inheritance can be managed until they reach the age of majority. A testamentary trust, unlike a living trust, is set up and funded as part of your will and comes into effect after your death. Be sure you have talked with those you want to serve as your children's guardian and any minors' trustee to make sure they are willing and able to take on these responsibilities.

✔ Prepare any necessary codicils to your will

It is a good idea to review your will every few years, especially whenever the tax laws change. Your personal or family circumstances may also have changed since you first drafted your will. Consult with your lawyer to make sure your will continues to express your estate plan.

A *codicil* is a document that amends your will. As circumstances change, such as a death, divorce, or birth in your family, you may want to change a part of your will. You may want to add a bequest for a new grandchild or change whom you want as your executor.

It can be easier to draft a codicil rather than rewriting and re-executing your entire will. But this is not a do-it-yourself project. Do not make any changes directly on your will. Strike outs, erasures, and any other markings on your will can have the devious effect of invalidating your will. A codicil must be executed with the same formality, number of witnesses, and notary requirements as your will.

✔ Consider if a living trust should be part of your estate plan

A living trust is a legal arrangement in which you transfer your interest in property so it can be managed for you. It is called a living trust because you create it while you are still alive. The trustee you select manages your trust assets while you are living as well as after your death. In addition to creating the trust document, you must also "fund" the trust by preparing deeds, retitling assets, reassigning brokerage accounts, or taking other steps to transfer ownership of the property you want in the trust. Because you must transfer legal ownership to the trust, the property in the trust no longer legally belongs to you and, therefore, is not part of your probate assets.

Every trust has three parties: the creator, the trustee, and the beneficiary or beneficiaries, although the same individual can be all three at the same time. Many people who create a living trust (called a settlor, grantor, or donor) name themselves as the trustee because they want to manage the trust as long as they can. They also name a successor trustee who takes over the trust management when the settlor no long is willing or able to be the trustee and then after the settlor's death. You can also name yourself as the principal trust beneficiary so you can receive the trust proceeds to support yourself while you are living. You would also name secondary beneficiaries with instructions on when and how the trust assets are to be managed and distributed after your death. In this way, your trust serves a very similar purpose to your will in identifying how any trust assets are distributed to the beneficiaries you have named. Because any assets you have transferred to the trust are not part of your probate estate, your trust, rather than your will, controls how those assets are distributed.

A trust can be an important component to your estate plan. Whether you should have a trust, in addition to your will, depends on many personal factors. If you have substantial property that you may not be able to manage if you become incapacitated, you may want to set up a trust. If a trustee manages your assets, your family may not need to have a guardian appointed to oversee your estate if you become mentally or physically unable to do so yourself. By placing real estate that you own in another state into a trust, you may be able to avoid going through probate in the other state.

You should discuss with your estate planner whether a trust would be appropriate in your circumstances and what assets might best be placed into a trust. Be sure to find out if placing your home in a living trust would jeopardize any homestead exemption, impact eligibility for Medicaid, or increase your property taxes. Putting property into a living trust does not reduce your income or estate taxes. It also does not protect your property from creditors. Because not all your property will be held by your trust, you will want to have a will to direct the distribution of any property that is not in your trust and that you have not otherwise planned for how it is to be inherited.

You may want to consider setting up a trust to provide for the care of your pets. According to the American Veterinary Medical Association, forty-four states have adopted pet trust laws. These laws specifically allow you to name your pet as a beneficiary of a trust so you can ensure that funds are available for its care.

✔ Select an agent to manage your financial affairs

A power of attorney can be one of the most useful documents that you can prepare, but it is effective only during your lifetime. By creating a power of attorney while you have the capacity to do so, you select the trustworthy individual—called your agent or attorney-in-fact—you want to manage your financial affairs if you become unable to do so yourself. A power of attorney can give you peace of mind that if you should become unable to take care of your business details for any reason, the person you choose will have the authority to start acting on your behalf.

You can determine what responsibilities and duties you want your agent to have. You may want to give your agent general powers to do everything that you could do, or you may want to give specific powers. Among the powers that you can delegate to another are the responsibility to manage your investments, pay your bills, collect your debts, sue on your behalf, sell your real estate, negotiate with insurance companies, sell your car, or have access to bank accounts. You may want your agent to sign your income tax returns, apply for benefits on your behalf, or make gifts to your favorite charities. If you want your agent to be able to make gifts of your money, you need to be very specific about how those gifts are to be made. You should design your power of attorney to fit your anticipated needs.

Powers of attorney can differ depending on when you want your agent to be able to act for you. A ***durable*** power of attorney begins when you sign and stays in effect for your lifetime—even after you become incapacitated—unless you cancel it. In most states you must put specific words in the document stating that you want your agent's powers to stay in effect even if you become incapacitated. If you want this feature, it's very important that you have these words in your document. In those states that have adopted the new Uniform Power of Attorney Act, you do not need to be concerned about including the "durable" language; the law presumes that you want your agent to act after you become incapacitated. Check with a lawyer in your state.

You can also state in your power of attorney that you want to delay the time when you want your agent to begin to act. This is called a ***springing*** power of attorney because the effectiveness of the document springs into effect at some time after you have signed the document. Your lawyer must carefully draft a springing power of attorney to avoid any difficulty in determining exactly when the springing event has happened.

Even if you sign a power of attorney, you can still manage your own affairs. You are not giving up anything. Think of a power of attorney as an extra set of car keys that you give to someone else. You have your own keys and determine when that extra set of keys can be used. When you can't or don't want to drive yourself, someone else has the keys to do the driving for you.

You can cancel, or revoke, a power of attorney at any time by tearing it up, signing a new one, or writing on it that you want to cancel it. You don't have to give any reason. If you do cancel, be sure to let your agent and anyone your agent has been dealing with know that you have cancelled your agent's authority. Just like your will, it is important to review your power of attorney every few years or when your circumstances change. If you move to a new state, it's a good idea to have a lawyer in that state review your powers of attorney.

All powers of attorney come to an end at your death. Your agent will have no authority to make any decisions after you die. Likewise, the executor you name in your will has no authority to act before your death.

Before deciding what powers you want your agent to have, carefully consider whom you want to be your agent. Select someone you trust completely and who can do the job. It is best to avoid someone who is ill, inexperienced in financial matters, or has a hard time managing his or her own money, or who for some other reason would not be able to carry out the responsibilities. Remember you are giving your agent the opportunity to act for you at a time when you may not be able to keep tabs on what the agent is doing. You may want to add ways for other people to check up on what your agent is doing when you cannot.

If you want your agent to have access to your bank account, be sure to get your bank's authorization forms and a signature card for your agent. Typically, a bank has its own form it wants your agent to sign before giving your agent access to a particular account. If you and your agent do not contact the bank before you become incapacitated, the bank may not honor checks or withdrawals your agent signs.

Giving your agent the authority to access your bank account is not the same as making someone a joint owner of the account. You'll want to make sure that you create the right kind of account so your agent has access to your funds to pay your bills but is not listed as an owner. Your bank may call this an agency, fiduciary, or convenience account.

✔ Prepare a letter of instruction

A letter of instruction serves as guidance to your personal representative and your family about matters they must attend to after your death and how you want specific personal possessions divided. This informal document can be attached to your will but is not an official part of it. You don't need a lawyer to prepare it. Although it doesn't carry the legal weight of a will and is in no way a substitute for one, a letter of instruction clarifies any special requests you want your family to carry out when you die. Think of it as a flexible, informal supplement to your will that covers more personal information than what is typically included in a will. You can easily change it as your circumstances or wishes change. All you need to do is sign and date your new letter.

Your letter of instructions can have two parts that do two different things. One part helps your family know how to find the information necessary to plan your funeral. You might include instructions about the type of funeral or memorial service you want, who should officiate, who you want as pallbearers, or what songs should—or should not—be sung. You need to let your family know about your plans with the funeral home and whether you have already paid for any of the arrangements. Describe the location of your pre-purchased burial plot or crypt and where you keep the plot deed. If you want to be cremated, your family needs to know where you want your ashes placed. Much of this information can be detailed in Chapter 10 of this book.

The other part of your letter of instruction may help eliminate any family feuds over who you want to receive your personal items. We all have heard stories of family fights erupting over how to divide family pictures, necklaces, the stamp collection, or the wedding gift from Aunt Sue. The items may not have monetary value, but getting them to the right person can make a big difference to you and to them.

If you want to make sure that your granddaughter gets the pearl necklace you got for your high school graduation, or you have already promised your best friend she gets your figurine collection, put your wishes in your letter. Be sure to leave instructions about care for your pets. If you have ideas or preferences as to who should get what, write it down.

You can make your letter personal, too. You can use it to send important messages to your survivors. You might include special hopes you have for your grandchild's education or the important values you want to pass on. This could be the place to tell your family something you never got around to saying. It can be whatever you want it to be. You may also want to consider preparing an ethical will discussed on page 218.

Your wishes can change over time. It is easy to revisit your instructions every couple of years or when your circumstances change. You don't have to follow any legal format. Always sign and date each revision to eliminate confusion over which is your most current statement. Just make sure your latest instructions are clear. Discard any older versions so there's no confusion about which version is the right one.

✔ Discuss your plan with those who need to know

Be sure you have talked with those you want to serve as the executor of your will, your children's guardian, your minors' trustee, your successor trustee, and your attorney-in-fact, to make sure they are willing and able to take on these responsibilities.

And be sure your loved ones know where all your documents are located. Some documents will be with your lawyer, others will be in your safe deposit box, and some will need to be on hand where your family can find them when decisions need to be made on your behalf.

Wills, Trusts, and Powers of Attorney Action Checklists

The checklists in Chapter 9 are set out in the following order:

- *Codicils*
- *Durable Power of Attorney*
- *Gifts*
- *Letter of Instruction*
- *Living Trust*
- *Will*
- *Wills, Trusts, and Powers of Attorneys: Other*

Codicils

☐ I have not executed any codicils.

☐ I have executed the following codicils:

Codicil date: _____

Lawyer's name: _____

Phone: _____ Email: _____

Address: _____

_____

Executor (if changed): _____

Phone: _____ Email: _____

Address: _____

_____

Witness's name: _____

Phone: _____ Email: _____

Address: _____

_____

Witness's name: _____

Phone: _____ Email: _____

Address: _____

_____

Durable Power of Attorney

☐   I do not have a durable power of attorney for financial management.

☐   I do have a durable power of attorney for financial management.

☐   I have discussed my expectations with my agent.

☐   My agent has a copy of my durable power of attorney.

Agent's name: _____

Phone: _____ Email:_____

Address: _____

_____

Gifts

☐   I have made no gifts in excess the annual exclusion amount ($14,000 in 2014).*

☐   I have made the following gifts in excess of the annual exclusion amount:

To Whom	Date	Gift	Value/Amount

* The annual gift exclusion changes from year to year. The annual exclusion applies to gifts to each donee. In other words, if you give each of your children $11,000 in 2002–2005, $12,000 in 2006–2008, $13,000 in 2009–2012, and $14,000 on or after January 1, 2013, the annual exclusion applies to each gift.

Letter of Instruction

    ☐ I do not have a letter of instruction.

    ☐ I do have a letter of instruction.

My letter of instruction is located: _____

I last updated my letter of instruction on: _____

Living Trust

☐   I do not have a living trust.

☐   I do have a living trust.

Lawyer's name:_____

Phone: _____ Email:_____

Address: _____

_____

Trustee's name: _____

Phone: _____ Email:_____

Address: _____

_____

Witness's name: _____

Phone: _____ Email:_____

Address: _____

_____

Witness's name: _____

Phone: _____ Email:_____

Address: _____

_____

The original of my living trust is located:_____

Will

☐   I do not have a will.

☐   I do have a will.

Executor's name: _____

Phone: _____   Email: _____

Address: _____

_____

Lawyer's name: _____

Phone: _____   Email: _____

Address: _____

_____

Witness's name: _____

Phone: _____   Email: _____

Address: _____

_____

Witness's name: _____

Phone: _____   Email: _____

Address: _____

_____

The original of my will is located: _____

Copies of my will are located: _____

Wills, Trusts, and Powers of Attorneys: Other

The following miscellaneous information about my estate planning may be of interest:

_____

_____

_____

_____

_____

_____

_____

_____

_____

_____

_____

_____

_____

_____

_____

_____

_____

_____

_____

_____

_____

_____

_____

_____

_____

_____

_____

CHAPTER 10
MEDICAL AND FINAL WISHES

Learn to wish that everything should come to pass
exactly as it does.

—Epictetus

One of the kindest things that you can do for your family members is to spare them the distress of facing decisions about your health care and your final arrangements without knowing your wishes. You can do this by making those decisions yourself and sharing them in this book.

Any time you become seriously ill—whatever your age—many decisions have to be made about the medical care that you receive. As long as you are able to communicate your wishes, health care providers look to you for answers about what treatment choices you want. In those situations when you cannot communicate your wishes, decisions still have to be made. Your family and health care providers want to respect your treatment preferences, but they need to know ahead of time how to make the decisions you want them to make. Advance care planning involves thinking about what treatments and health care you do or do not want, communicating your thoughts to those who will be called upon to make decisions on your behalf, and finally, putting those wishes down on paper in the appropriate legal forms.

In addition to knowing your wishes for your health care, your family members will need to make many decisions at the time of your death. You will be giving them a precious gift if you relieve them of any uncertainty about your wishes. By indicating on the checklists in this chapter what you want and the plans you have in place, your loved ones will be able to act with confidence that they are doing the right thing.

You may want a simple ceremony that celebrates your life or a more elaborate memorial service. If you are a veteran, you may want a military bugler with burial in a national cemetery. Many people have firm opinions about whether a casket should be open or closed.

Also, if you have pre-paid for any part of your funeral or burial, your family members need to know about the contract so they don't have to pay unnecessarily for anything you have already paid for. Decisions concerning the care of your body, including whether you want to be cremated or embalmed, are time sensitive. Your family also has to know promptly upon your death if you have already made arrangements with a medical school to donate your body for medical research or if you wish to be an organ donor.

My To-Do Checklist

Done   Need to Do

Done	Need to Do	
☐	☐	Select the person you want to be your health care agent
☐	☐	Consider preparing an ethical will
☐	☐	Prepare an organ donor card
☐	☐	Plan the disposition of your body
☐	☐	Plan your funeral
☐	☐	Consider options for paying for your funeral
☐	☐	Plan your final resting place
☐	☐	Know your veterans burial benefits
☐	☐	Complete the checklists for Chapter 10

✔ **Select the person you want to be your health care agent**

Health care directives

An advance directive is a legally accepted means for you to convey to your family and health care providers the types of care you would want in the event you are unable to communicate and who you want to make decisions about that care when you cannot.

Most people have heard of a *living will*, yet it's only half the legal instruction that makes up an advance directive. A living will outlines the treatments you would or would not want if you are unable to communicate and your death is imminent, or if you're permanently unconscious, in a vegetative state, or in the end-stage of a chronic condition such as Alzheimer's disease. You may want to talk with your doctor about what are these life-limiting conditions.

In most states, the law restricts the circumstances under which a living will is effective. Typically you can use it to document your wishes concerning specific end-of-life treatments. While it is crucial that your family and doctors understand your preferences concerning life-prolonging treatments, such as use of respirators, cardiopulmonary resuscitation, or intravenous nutrition or hydration, you may want to consider additional advance directives.

The second part of an advance directive is the selection of a health care agent who can speak for you if you are unable to do so. This is also referred to as appointing a health care proxy or signing a ***durable power of attorney for health care***. In your advance directive, you can give your agent broad authority to make any health care decision you specify, not about just life-prolonging treatments. You can set down any guidance or instructions you want your agent and your health care team to follow. And, perhaps more importantly, you can have someone who will speak for you and get necessary information from your health care providers to make the decisions you would want to be made. By having your preferences in writing and someone to speak up on your behalf, you can help your family make difficult decisions and make sure your personal values are respected.

Your agent should be someone who knows you and understands your wishes about medical treatments. You can authorize him or her to make decisions in situations you might not have anticipated. Your agent can talk with your health care providers about your changing medical condition and authorize treatment or have it withdrawn as circumstances change. In the sometimes bewildering medical system, it is good to have someone in charge who can advocate for you. If health care providers resist following your wishes, your agent can stand up for what you want and take any other necessary steps to see that your wishes are honored. This includes changing doctors or hospitals if necessary to get the care you want.

When selecting your health care agent, you should choose someone you trust and who will be there for you now and well into the future. You will need to feel comfortable talking with him or her about your end-of-life care and confident that he or she will follow your wishes even if they are not similar to his or her own. Your agent should be able to be assertive, if necessary, when talking with health care professionals. Your choice also needs to meet your state's criteria for health care agents. Most states exclude some categories of people who can serve as agents—such as your doctor, the administrator of the nursing home where you are living, or someone who works in your nursing home.

The first step in preparing an advance directive is to consider what you may want for medical care in the future. For many, this is not a simple step. It can be hard to foresee what your medical needs or problems might be at some unknown point in the future. You may want to talk with your family, doctor, spiritual advisers, or others who might be helpful in talking through serious medical issues and what brings quality to your life. The Five Wishes advance directive form (www.agingwithdignity.org/five-wishes.php) may be helpful in starting and structuring important conversations about the medical care you wish to have. The American Bar Association also has a kit that is very helpful in discussing with doctors and family your spiritual values, personal priorities, and more at www.americanbar.org /aging/toolkit/.

The next step is preparing your advance directive. You don't need a lawyer to draft this document. You can find state-specific forms at www.aarp.org/advancedirectives and links to other information about advance directives at http://ambar.org/HealthCarePOA. Many elder law attorneys will help you prepare your advance directives as part of estate and advance care planning. Most hospitals, area agencies on aging, and medical societies also provide free forms.

Perhaps even more important than signing the document is the conversations you need to have with your health care agent. Your agent needs to understand what is important to you for your quality of life and the kind of medical care you would or would not want to have. Think of your advance directive as a written record of the conversations you have had with your agent about how you want to live up until the moment you die. Having your preferences in writing can be backup support for your agent and provide assurance that your wishes are known.

Your agent and your health care providers need to have copies of your advance directives. You may also wish to carry a wallet card that indicates you have an advance directive and how to get in touch with your agent.

✔ **Consider preparing an ethical will**

Ethical Will

Ethical wills may be one of the most cherished and meaningful gifts you can leave to your family. They are a way to share with your family, friends, and future generations your values, blessings, life's lessons, hopes and dreams for the future, love and forgiveness. Preparing an ethical will is an opportunity to put down on paper what you hold dear—your memories, insights, and special wisdom that you don't want to be lost or forgotten. You may also want to make a video or audio recording of your ethical will as a cherished legacy for later generations.

Ethical wills are not new. They are an ancient tradition for passing on personal values, beliefs, blessings, and advice to future generations. Initially, ethical wills were transmitted orally. Over time, they evolved into written documents. Ethical wills are not considered legal documents, unlike your living will and your last will and testament.

Dr. Barry Baines, author of *Ethical Wills: Putting Your Values on Paper*, suggests the following personal reasons for writing an ethical will.

- We all want to be remembered, and we all will leave something behind.
- If we don't tell our stories, no one else will and they will be lost forever.

- It helps us identify what we value most and what we stand for.

- By articulating what we value now, we can take steps to ensure the continuation of those values for future generations.

- You learn a lot about yourself in the process of writing an ethical will.

- It helps us come to terms with our mortality by creating something of meaning that will live on after we are gone.

- It provides a sense of completion in our lives.

To help you get started, you can find examples of ethical wills and tips on how to prepare one at ethicalwill.com/examples.html or www.personallegacyadvisors.com/know ledge-base/ethical-wills/contemporary-examples-of-ethical-wills.

✔ Prepare an organ donor card

Do you wish to share the gift of your organs or tissues with someone needing a transplant? These donations have saved or improved thousands of lives at absolutely no cost to the donor. Yet there is always a very long list of patients waiting for organ transplants. According to the U.S. Department of Health and Human Services, eighteen patients die each day because of the shortage of available donated organs.

If you do wish to give this gift, you need to sign and carry an organ donation card. In some states, you can indicate your wish to be an organ donor on your driver's license. Most, but not all, states have an organ donation registry. You can find out if your state does at www.organdonor.gov/donor/registry.html. Sign up on your state's registry so your wishes can be honored.

Most organ donations are made after a person has been declared brain dead following an accident, heart attack, or stroke. The organs or tissues are removed through a surgical procedure. Most transplanted organs must be used within hours of the donation, while tissue donations of corneas, heart valves, skin, and bones can be preserved and stored in tissue banks. After the removal procedures, your body can be buried or cremated as though it were intact.

If you wish to make a *whole body donation* to a medical school or research facility, you need to make arrangements with the school or research entity before you die. You can find a list of anatomical research programs at www.med.ufl.edu/anatbd/usprograms.html. Be sure to talk with your family members about your donation wish so they will know the specific instructions for how to transfer your body. Typically the facility will cremate your body at no expense and deliver your ashes as you instruct.

✔ **Plan the disposition of your body**

You will need to decide what you wish to have done with your body after your death. Your choices may include being embalmed to delay decomposition of your body, a natural burial without embalming, burial in a coffin in a cemetery or in a crypt in a mausoleum, or cremation. If you prefer cremation, your ashes may be buried in an urn at a cemetery, placed in a columbarium, or scattered at the location of your choice.

You can choose whether you want your body to be embalmed or cremated. Those who wish to be cremated can forego being embalmed. With direct cremation, your body would go directly from the place of death to the crematory. Before cremation, an official will need to prepare a death certificate and obtain a cremation permit. Typically, your spouse or next of kin will need to sign a consent about the disposition of your body. You may want to sign a pre-need authorization for cremation, especially if you have no spouse or close family. In this document, you appoint the person you want to consent to your cremation and to receive your ashes. A funeral home or crematory should be able to give you a form for you to sign so you can make sure your wishes to be cremated are carried out.

Every state has regulations concerning the scattering of ashes, so check with your state agency that regulates burials. The scattering of ashes at sea must be done three nautical miles from land and the Environmental Protection Agency needs notice within thirty days of the burial.

More people are considering natural or "green" burials. With natural burial, your body would be promptly buried, without embalming, in the ground in a biodegradable coffin made of cardboard or bamboo or in a shroud. Or you could have a tree or shrub planted instead of a stone grave marker, or request that instead of flowers, gifts could be made to your favorite charity.

Those of the Jewish faith may have special rituals for washing the body, staying with the body until burial, and promptly burying the body without embalming.

Because of the many options, be sure your family knows of your wishes.

✔ **Plan your funeral**

How do you wish your death to be commemorated? Depending on your family and cultural or religious traditions, you may wish no service or ceremony, a lively gathering of family and friends to celebrate your life, a memorial service, a viewing at a mortuary, a wake, or a religious service in your place of worship. A funeral generally means that the body of the deceased is present, while a memorial service is held after the body has been buried or has been cremated.

A funeral director can help you plan for whatever type of commemoration you wish. You can discuss ahead of time the type of casket you would prefer, as well as other arrangements for any service or ceremony. Funeral directors must give you written price lists that tell you the costs for body preparation and transportation, caskets or urns, grave liners or "outer burial containers," and other services.

With the price lists in hand, you can comparison shop among several funeral homes to make sure you get the arrangements exactly as you desire and have a better idea about the range of costs. Keep in mind that you can choose where you purchase your casket. You can even shop for one online.

A funeral director can also help you make arrangements for the type of grave marker or headstone you prefer. Headstones typically extend above the ground to identify the person buried. Grave markers lay flat on the ground. Some cemeteries or memorial parks require grave markers to make it easier to care for the grounds. You can indicate on the Burial Checklist the inscription you want on your headstone or grave marker.

✔ **Consider options for paying for your funeral**

Many funeral establishments let you pay a fixed price now for your funeral. Pre-paying fixes the costs at today's prices for your choice of a coffin and other services that may cost more in the future. Equally important, making your own financial arrangements gives you the peace of mind that your family will not have this financial burden.

Before pre-paying for your funeral with a funeral director, get confirmation in writing about how your financial investment will be protected. You want to be assured that your money is in safe hands and your pre-need contract will be honored as much as a decade or two in the future. With most pre-need contracts you turn over a sum of money, either a lump sum or in installment payments. Your money is then placed in trust held by a third-party trustee or used to purchase an insurance policy. The trustee or insurance company is responsible for managing the money until it is time to pay the funeral home for the goods and services you listed in your contract. Ask whether your funds will be securely placed in a trust held by a financially sound third party or used to purchase an insurance policy.

You will also want to inquire about the portability of your contract if you should move to another location and no longer want your funeral where you used to live. If your plans change or the funeral home changes hands, you'll want to be able to transfer the contract to a different funeral home.

Before paying for a pre-need contract, check with your state's attorney general or board of funeral directors to learn how pre-need contracts are regulated in your state. Your family will need to know if you have a pre-need contract, so include the details on the Funeral Checklist.

There are other options for making sure your family is not saddled with the expenses for your funeral. Funerals are expensive—on average, $7,000—along with the emotional toll when someone dies. You may wish to purchase a life insurance policy that would cover the anticipated funeral costs, or invest your money in a certificate of deposit or in a savings account designated to cover these expenses. With options like these, you will know that the money will be available to your family, but you remain in control of the money as your plans for your final arrangements change.

✔ Plan your final resting place

If you wish your body to be buried, you will need to purchase a lot at a cemetery or a niche in a mausoleum. You can purchase just a single lot or a number of lots in a block where other family members would also be buried. When purchasing a cemetery lot, ask about any additional charges for the opening and closing and perpetual care of the site. You should receive a deed to the land, or plot, that you have purchased. The cost of cemetery lots varies significantly depending on where you wish to be buried. It is essential that your relatives know if you have purchased a cemetery plot or crypt in a mausoleum so they can make the correct arrangements. Be sure to record that information on the Burial Checklist.

✔ Know your veterans burial benefits

If you are an eligible U.S. military veteran, the U.S. Department of Veterans Affairs (VA) provides a bundle of benefits at the time of your burial. The available benefits depend upon your length of service, the era during which you served, whether you are disabled, whether the disability was caused by active service, and many other criteria. Be sure to indicate on the Veterans Burial Benefits Checklist if you want any of these benefits.

Family members applying for VA benefits need a copy of your service record, or your DD-214. The DD-214 will specify that you were on active military duty and show that your release from active duty was under other than dishonorable conditions. You can get this very important record at www.archives.gov/veterans/military-service-records/.

> **Burial flag:** A U.S. flag may be issued to drape over your casket. After the funeral service, the flag will be given to your next of kin or close friend or associate. Flags are issued at any VA office and most local post offices. A Presidential Memorial Certificate is also available at no cost to the family.

> **Burial in a national cemetery:** Burial in a national cemetery is open to all members of the Armed Forces and veterans who have met minimum active service duty requirements and were discharged under conditions other than dishonorable. Your spouse, widow or widower, minor children, and, under certain conditions, unmarried adult children are also eligible for burial in a national cemetery. In most cases, one gravesite is provided for the burial of all eligible family members and a single headstone or marker is provided. When both you and your spouse are veterans, you can request two gravesites and two headstones or markers. Certain members of the Armed Forces reserve components may also be eligible for burial.

In each instance, space must be available. There is no charge for the grave plot, its opening and closing, a grave liner, or perpetual care.

Headstone or marker: Eligible veterans can receive a government headstone or marker to be placed at their grave, whether a national cemetery or elsewhere, at any cemetery around the world. Even if the grave was previously marked, you can obtain a government headstone. A headstone or marker is automatically furnished if burial is in a national cemetery. Otherwise, you must apply to the VA. The VA will ship the headstone or marker, without charge, to the person or firm designated on the application. The VA will also furnish a medallion, on request, to place on an existing headstone or marker that indicates that the person was a veteran. You must pay the cost of setting the headstone or marker, or attaching the medallion.

Military honors: By law every eligible veteran may receive a military funeral honors ceremony, to include folding and presenting the U.S. burial flag and the playing of Taps. A military funeral honors detail consists of two or more uniformed military persons, with at least one being a member of the veteran's branch of the Armed Forces. The Department of Defense program, "Honoring Those Who Served," calls for funeral directors to request military funeral honors on behalf of the family. Veterans' organizations may assist in providing military funeral honors. In support of this program, VA national cemetery staff can help coordinate military funeral honors either at a national or a private cemetery. For more information go to www.cem.va.gov/military_funeral_honors.asp.

Reimbursement for funeral or burial expenses: The VA is authorized to pay an allowance toward your funeral and burial expenses. If it was a service-related death, the VA will pay up to $2,000 toward your burial expenses. If you are to be buried in a VA national cemetery, some or all of the cost of transporting your body to the cemetery may be reimbursed. For a nonservice-related death, the VA will pay up to $300 toward your burial and funeral expenses and a $300 plot-interment allowance. If the death happens while you were in a VA hospital or under VA-contracted nursing home care, some or all of the costs for transporting your remains may be reimbursed.

A note about bereavement fares: Most airlines used to offer bereavement fares so family members could save on the price of a ticket when they needed to fly on short notice because of an emergency or death in the family. Unfortunately, many airlines no longer offer bereavement fares. Check the airline's policy before booking. Online sites with last-minute deals, such as Hotwire, Kayak, Orbitz, Priceline, or Travelocity, may have lower prices.

Medical and Final Wishes Action Checklists

The checklists in Chapter 10 are set out in the following order:

- *Burial*
- *Celebration of Life*
- *Charities*
- *Cremation*
- *Donation of Organs and Tissues*
- *Entombment*
- *Ethical Will/Legacy Documents*
- *Final Wishes*
- *Funeral*
- *Health Care Directives*
- *Items to Destroy*
- *Letters to Friends and Relatives*
- *Memorial Service*
- *Obituary*
- *People to Contact*
- *Pet Care*
- *Veterans Burial Benefits*
- *Whole Body Donation*
- *Final Wishes: Other*

Burial

- ☐ I do not wish to be buried.
- ☐ I wish to be buried.
- ☐ I do not own a cemetery lot.
- ☐ I own a cemetery lot.

The ownership of the cemetery lot is in the name of: _____

The lot is located at:

Cemetery: _____

Section: _____ Lot: _____

Address: _____

_____

Other description:

_____

_____

_____

_____

_____

_____

_____

_____

_____

_____

_____

_____

_____

_____

_____

Location of deed: _____

☐ I would like to have a grave marker.

☐ I would like to have a grave marker furnished by the Department of Veterans Affairs.

☐ I would like to have a service medallion furnished by the Department of Veterans Affairs.

I would like the following words to be placed on grave marker:

_____
_____
_____
_____

I would like the following type of casket:

_____
_____
_____

Other burial instructions:

_____
_____
_____
_____
_____
_____
_____
_____
_____
_____
_____
_____
_____

Celebration of Life

☐   I do not want a celebration of life ceremony.

☐   I want a celebration of life ceremony.

☐   I have made prearrangements for a celebration of life ceremony.

Type of celebration: _____

People to invite:

_____

_____

_____

_____

_____

_____

Arrangement details:

Place: _____

Time: _____

Food or beverage suggestions:

_____

_____

_____

_____

_____

Entertainment or music suggestions:

_____

_____

_____

_____

    ☐ I have created music for the celebration.

    ☐ I have created a video for the celebration.

    ☐ I have created photos for the celebration.

    ☐ I have other requests for the celebration:

_____

_____

_____

_____

Notes for music:

_____

_____

_____

_____

Notes for photos:

_____

_____

_____

_____

Notes for video:

_____

_____

_____

_____

Charities

☐   I do not want any memorial donations or gifts to charities.

☐   I would appreciate memorial donations or gifts to the following charities:

Charity name: _____

Contact information: _____

Website: _____

Significance to me: _____

Charity name: _____

Contact information: _____

Website: _____

Significance to me: _____

Charity name: _____

Contact information: _____

Website: _____

Significance to me: _____

Charity name: _____

Contact information: _____

Website: _____

Significance to me: _____

Charity name: _____

Contact information: _____

Website: _____

Significance to me: _____

Cremation

☐ I do not want my body to be cremated.

☐ I want my body to be cremated.

☐ I want my body to be cremated followed by a memorial service.

☐ I want my body to be cremated followed by a celebration of life service.

Following my cremation, I wish my ashes to be disbursed as follows:

☐ To be scattered:

_____

☐ To be placed in an urn and buried or entombed:

_____

☐ Other:

_____

☐ To be handled as my family sees fit.

****

☐ I have not made prearrangements for my cremation.

☐ I have made the following prearrangements for my cremation:

Company: _____

Address: _____

_____

Phone: _____ Website: _____

The contract is located: _____

Donation of Organs and Tissues

☐   I do not wish to donate any organs or tissues.

☐   I wish to donate any needed organs or tissues.

☐   My blood type is: _____

☐   I wish to donate only the following organs or tissues:

Organs:

☐   Heart

☐   Kidneys

☐   Liver

☐   Lungs

☐   Pancreas

☐   Other_____

Tissues:

☐   Blood vessels

☐   Bone

☐   Cartilage

☐   Corneas

☐   Heart valves

☐   Inner ear

☐   Intestines

☐   Skin

☐   Other _____

****

☐   I have not prepared a uniform donor card.

☐   I have a uniform donor card.

☐   I have registered with my state's organ donation registry at this website: _____

☐   My uniform donor card is located: _____

Entombment

- ☐ I do not wish to be entombed.
- ☐ I want to be entombed.
- ☐ I do not own a crypt.
- ☐ I own the following crypt:

The ownership of the crypt is in the name of: _____

The crypt is located at:

Church/Mausoleum/Columbarium: _____

Address: _____

_____

Space #:_____

Other description:

_____

_____

Location of deed: _____

I would like the following words to be placed on the crypt:

_____

_____

Other instructions:

_____

_____

_____

_____

_____

_____

Ethical Will/Legacy Documents

☐ I have not created any legacy documents.

☐ I have created an ethical will.

☐ I have created the following legacy documents:

Ethical will:

_____

_____

_____

Books:

_____

_____

_____

Pamphlets:

_____

_____

_____

Videos:

_____

_____

_____

Other:

_____

_____

_____

Please distribute them as follows:

_____

_____

_____

Final Wishes

I wish to:

- ☐ Be embalmed
- ☐ Be an organ donor (see the Donation of Organs and Tissues Checklist)
- ☐ Have my body bequeathed to a medical school (see the Whole Body Donation Checklist)
- ☐ Have my body buried in the earth (see the Burial Checklist)
- ☐ Have my body entombed in a mausoleum (see the Entombment Checklist)
- ☐ Be cremated (see the Cremation Checklist)
- ☐ Other: _____

****

I wish to have:

- ☐ A funeral service (body present) (see the Funeral Checklist)
- ☐ A memorial service (body not present) (see the Memorial Service Checklist)
- ☐ A celebration of life service
- ☐ No service
- ☐ A graveside service
- ☐ I would like a U.S. flag covering my coffin
- ☐ I would like to have military funeral honors
- ☐ Other: _____

****

My preferences are as follows:

_____
_____
_____
_____
_____
_____
_____

Funeral

☐   I do not want a funeral.

☐   I want a funeral.

☐   I have not made funeral prearrangements.

☐   I have a pre-need contract and have pre-paid for some or all of my funeral.

☐   I have made the following prearrangements:

_____

_____

_____

_____

_____

The pre-need contract is located: _____

I wish the service to be for:

☐   Friends and relatives

☐   Private

☐   Other: _____

I wish the casket to be:

☐   Closed

☐   Open

☐   I prefer to wear: _____

Funeral establishment: _____

Address: _____

_____

Phone: _____ Email: _____

House of worship:

_____

_____

_____

Religious leader/Officiant/Clergy:

_____

_____

Speakers/Readers:

_____

_____

_____

_____

Ushers/Pallbearers:

_____

_____

_____

_____

Favorite scripture, psalms, poems, readings:

_____

_____

_____

_____

Special hymns, music, musicians, soloists:

_____

_____

_____

_____

Health Care Directives

☐ I do not have a durable power of attorney for health care.

☐ I have a durable power of attorney for health care.

☐ I have talked with my health care agent about my medical preferences.

☐ I do not have a living will.

☐ I have a living will.

Health care agent's name: _____

Phone: _____ Email: _____

Address: _____

_____

☐ I have given copies of my health care directives to the following:

Health care agent: _____

Physician: _____

Physician: _____

Physician: _____

Hospital: _____

Home health care agency: _____

Residential care facility: _____

Other: _____

Items to Destroy

Please destroy the following documents upon my death:

Item: _____

_____

_____

Location: _____

Item: _____

_____

_____

Location: _____

Item: _____

_____

_____

Location: _____

Item: _____

_____

_____

Location: _____

Item: _____

_____

_____

Location: _____

Item: _____

_____

_____

Location: _____

Letters to Friends and Relatives

☐   I do not have any letters for friends or relatives.

☐   I have prepared letters for friends and relatives as follows:

Person:_____

Address: _____

_____

Letter location: _____

Person:_____

Address: _____

_____

Letter location: _____

Person:_____

Address: _____

_____

Letter location: _____

Person:_____

Address: _____

_____

Letter location: _____

Person:_____

Address: _____

_____

Letter location: _____

Person:_____

Address: _____

_____

Letter location: _____

Memorial Service

☐ I do not want a memorial service.

☐ I want a memorial service.

I wish the service to be for:

☐ Friends and relatives

☐ Private

☐ Other: _____

☐ I wish to have the following at my memorial service:

House of worship:

_____

_____

_____

Religious leader/Officiant/Clergy:

_____

_____

Speakers/Readers:

_____

_____

_____

_____

_____

Ushers/Pallbearers:

_____

_____

_____

_____

_____

_____

Favorite scripture, psalms, poems, readings:

_____

_____

_____

_____

_____

_____

_____

_____

_____

Special hymns, music, musicians, soloists:

_____

_____

_____

_____

_____

_____

_____

_____

_____

_____

_____

Obituary

☐ I have not written my own obituary.

☐ I have written my own obituary.

My obituary is located: _____

I would like my obituary to appear in the following newspapers:

Newspaper name: _____

Newspaper website: _____ _____

I would like my obituary posted online at: _____

I would like the following information to appear in my obituary:

_____

_____

_____

_____

_____

_____

_____

_____

_____

_____

_____

_____

_____

_____

_____

_____

_____

_____

_____

_____

People to Contact

Please inform the following people of my death:

Name: _____

Relationship: _____

Phone: _____ Email: _____

Address: _____

_____

Name: _____

Relationship: _____

Phone: _____ Email: _____

Address: _____

_____

Name: _____

Relationship: _____

Phone: _____ Email: _____

Address: _____

_____

Name: _____

Relationship: _____

Phone: _____ Email: _____

Address: _____

_____

Name: _____

Relationship: _____

Phone: _____ Email: _____

Address: _____

_____

Pet Care

- ☐ I do not have any pets.
- ☐ I have not made arrangements for the care of my pets.
- ☐ I have made arrangements for the care of my pets.
- ☐ I have not made financial arrangements for the care of my pets.
- ☐ I have made financial arrangements for the care of my pets.

I have made the following arrangements for the care of my pets:

_____

_____

_____

_____

_____

_____

_____

_____

_____

I have made the following financial arrangements for the care of my pets:

_____

_____

_____

_____

_____

_____

_____

_____

_____

_____

_____

_____

_____

Veterans Burial Benefits

- ☐ I did not serve in the U.S. military.
- ☐ I served in the U.S. military.
- ☐ I or other family members may be eligible for veterans benefits.
- ☐ I have a copy of my DD-214.
- ☐ I want a burial flag for my casket.
- ☐ I want burial in a national cemetery.
- ☐ I want a veteran's headstone.
- ☐ I want military honors at the burial.

Name I served under while in the military:

_____

      First   *Middle*   *Last*

My DD-213 is located: _____

I entered active service on: _____

I was separated from active service on: _____

Branch: _____

Grade or rank: _____

National Guard: _____

Reserves: _____

Whole Body Donation

☐ I do not wish to donate my body for medical science.

☐ I have not made prearrangements with any medical school or research organization.

☐ I have made the following prearrangements with the following medical school or research organization:

Medical school: _____

Address: _____

_____

Phone: _____

Contact person: _____

Research organization: _____

Address: _____

_____

Phone: _____

Contact person: _____

Medical and Final Wishes: Other

The following miscellaneous information about my final wishes may be of interest:

_____

_____

_____

_____

_____

_____

_____

_____

_____

_____

_____

_____

_____

_____

_____

_____

_____

_____

_____

_____

_____

_____

_____

_____

_____

_____

_____

_____

_____

_____

_____

_____

_____

_____